BORDEAUX

AND ITS WINES

BORDEAUX

AND ITS WINES

ROBERT JOSEPH

PHOTOGRAPHY BY MAX ALEXANDER

DUNCAN BAIRD PUBLISHERS
LONDON

Bordeaux and its Wines
An appreciation by Robert Joseph
Photography by Max Alexander

Distributed in the USA and Canada by
Sterling Publishing Co., Inc.
387 Park Avenue South
New York, NY 10016-8810

First published in the UK and
Ireland in 2003 by
Duncan Baird Publishers Ltd
Sixth Floor, Castle House
75–76 Wells Street
London W1T 3QH

Managing Editor: Judy Barratt
Editor: James Hodgson
Managing Designer: Manisha Patel
Designer: Megan Smith
Commissioned maps: Neil Gower

Library of Congress Cataloging-in-Publication
Data available

10 9 8 7 6 5 4 3 2 1

ISBN-10: 1-84483-605-3
ISBN-13: 978-1-84483-605-5

Typeset in Mrs Eaves
Colour reproduction by Scanhouse, Malaysia
Printed in China by Imago

For information about custom editions, special
sales, premium and corporate purchases, please
contact Sterling Special Sales Department at
800-805-5489 or specialsales@sterlingpub.com.

NOTES
The following abbreviations are used in this book:
bce Before the Common Era (the equivalent of bc)
ce Common Era (the equivalent of ad)

Measurements are shown in metric units —
below are approximate imperial equivalents:
1 hectare = 2.5 acres
1 kilogram = 2.2 pounds
1 kilometre = 0.6 of a mile

Captions to photographs pp.1–5:
p.1 Vineyard on the road between Bourg and Blaye
p.2 Vineyard near Puisseguin
pp.4–5 Panorama near Targon (Entre-Deux-Mers)

CONTENTS

Foreword by Hugh Johnson 6

Author's introduction 8

About Bordeaux 12

CHAPTER ONE THE CITY OF BORDEAUX 18

CHAPTER TWO THE MÉDOC 30

CHAPTER THREE GRAVES AND PESSAC-LÉOGNAN 52

CHAPTER FOUR SAUTERNES AND BARSAC 74

CHAPTER FIVE ENTRE-DEUX-MERS 82

CHAPTER SIX LIBOURNE, ST ÉMILION AND POMEROL 96

CHAPTER SEVEN NORTHWARD FROM POMEROL 118

PRACTICAL REFERENCE
Choosing wine in Bordeaux 130
Le terroir 133
Directory of recommended châteaux 136

Acknowledgments 144

CHÂTEAU COS D'ESTOURNEL, ONE OF THE MOST MEMORABLE IMAGES OF BORDEAUX — A MOCK-ORIENTAL FAÇADE BUILT AS A FOLLY BY ITS WELL-TRAVELLED OWNER, AND THE SOURCE OF ONE OF THE FINEST WINES IN THE MÉDOC.

FOREWORD BY HUGH JOHNSON

Bordeaux. It is a resonant word. It names a city, a region and a wine – no, many wines, whose style and quality have made them, over many centuries, as much an icon of European culture as gothic architecture or Italian gardens. To be recognizable and recognized by the population of a continent, if not the whole world, argues a consistency, and an originality, that very few cities, regions and their products have ever attained.

No wonder it attracts the curious. I was drawn to Bordeaux, just as Robert Joseph was, but maybe ten years earlier, to look for its enigmatic soul. The wines that still fascinate us both range from the forgettably pedestrian to the awe-inspiring, to tastes that become markers in your sensual life and never leave you.

Can one identity embrace them all? What can they have in common? In an almost mystical way it is the taste of this Atlantic shore. Yes, you taste the fruit, you are aware of the grapes in a glass of Bordeaux – though less so than in a glass of Burgundy. But first you are made aware of the stones, gravel, grit, clay or limestone that stored the water that turned into wine. It is the sense of place that unites such disparate drinks.

And the place? Bordeaux the city has the cool glamour of a northern port perched at the edge of the Mediterranean world. Bordeaux is austere; the stony perspectives of its streets are as strictly disciplined as the endless vinerows of its hinterland. Its history and fortunes are more closely allied to northern Europe than to the rest of France. England is nearer by sea than Paris, and Edinburgh, Hamburg and the ports of Scandinavia and the Baltic are open to the same grey water that reflects its golden stone.

Product and place together define a whole culture, complex and long-simmered. Between the producers of Bordeaux, its traders and their customers across the waves there are assumptions, methods of working, values that can be disputed because they are so strongly shared.

Can they be simply stated? Not simply, but vividly, clearly and usefully. As Robert Joseph does in this book.

AUTHOR'S INTRODUCTION

Everyone who enjoys wine finds his or her way to the subject through their own particular door. In my case, it all began, as a child, with a sublime sip of Château d'Yquem which was, in turn, followed by a series of similarly small sips of red wine from some of the most famous châteaux in Bordeaux.

I was given this extraordinarily privileged vinous education over a number of years by the waiters in my parents' English country hotel where I spent most of my childhood. Noticing my precocious interest in all these mysterious liquids that the grown-ups seemed to enjoy and take so seriously, Mario or Jean-Paul or Manuel would hand me a glass containing a few drops from the bottle they had been pouring into a decanter or that had been left by a customer at the end of a meal. In those days, more often than not, the wine in question would have been Bordeaux, a region I soon associated with flavours that were fascinating and enigmatic, and, on occasion, quite challenging. Some reminded me

unpleasantly of tea I had allowed to grow cold, leaving my mouth feeling as though it had been on the receiving end of a heavy punch; others were rich and fruity and curiously almost sweet while lacking any trace of sugar. Others, still, seemed to smell of the countryside in the spring or autumn, or of woodsmoke and tar, or of the farm at the end of the lane.

Even at that early age, I was aware that the secret of all these stern, straight-sided, high-shouldered bottles and their contents lay in the place they came from. So, almost as soon as the law allowed, armed with a couple of books, I set out for France in a little Austin Mini, on an exploratory tour that began with the Loire, Burgundy and the Rhône and came to a lengthy climax in Bordeaux. I don't know quite what I expected to find. There would of course be the châteaux whose images had featured on so many of the labels, but what would the vineyards surrounding them look like? And what kind of places were Bordeaux, St Émilion and Pauillac?

SOME OF THE FINEST WINES IN BORDEAUX: CHÂTEAUX MONTROSE, MARGAUX, LATOUR, MOUTON-ROTHSCHILD AND LAFITE-ROTHSCHILD FROM THE MÉDOC; PÉTRUS FROM POMEROL AND HAUT-BRION FROM PESSAC-LÉOGNAN.

On that first trip at the beginning of the 1970s, despite spending a week driving to almost every corner of the region, I never did find Bordeaux. What I discovered was a collection of quite different landscapes and towns. Some of the vines grew on land that was almost flat, while others covered hills not unlike the ones I had seen in Burgundy. A few were even planted on slopes almost as steep as some in Alsace and the Rhône. There were vineyards that ran alongside rivers, and plots that were tucked away magically between patches of forest. The precious soil of which I had read so much, even to my untutored eye, varied from fine brown dust to chunky-white and ash-grey gravel, and some vineyards were scattered with what looked like shiny quartz jewels.

The châteaux were a gloriously diverse collection too, ranging from the unashamed majesty of Margaux, and Château St-Georges in St-Georges-St-Émilion, to the medieval castles of Issan, Yquem and Lamarque and the disconcertingly humble cottages of Pomerol producing wines such as La Fleur de Gay. The city of Bordeaux itself struck this particular adolescent visitor as rather a forbidding place whose buildings seemed to be the architectural embodiment of men in business suits. Pauillac, by contrast, reminded me of the sleepy river resorts I associated with the French impressionists, while the tapestry of warm stone walls and terracotta roofs of St Émilion might easily have been imported directly from Tuscany.

I have been back to Bordeaux countless times since to taste its new and old wines, to revise those initial impressions and to continue my lifelong search for the region. Even now when I suppose I ought to know better, I invariably get lost among the vineyards somewhere or take a wrong turning in one of the towns and villages — only to happen upon yet another piece of the Bordeaux puzzle.

Researching and writing this book and working with a photographer as talented as Max Alexander has been a delight. I hope you enjoy the pictures and the words as much as we enjoyed producing them.

Robert Joseph

CHÂTEAU BONNET: A VERY GRAND CHÂTEAU IN THE ENTRE-DEUX-MERS, A LESS THAN GRAND PART OF BORDEAUX — AND THE SOURCE OF SOME OF THE MOST RELIABLE, HIGH-QUALITY, GREAT-VALUE WINES IN THE REGION.

ABOUT BORDEAUX

Bordeaux is a chimera: a city that's also a region; a land of vineyards that's rich in pine forests, sandy beaches and scrubland; a collection of 8,000 wine-producing "châteaux" some of which barely qualify as cottages; an annual flood of wines that run the gamut from dire to divine. Bordeaux is all of these things and more, and to consider the components separately is rather like trying to unpick the patches from a quilt. Without at least a cursory knowledge of the environment and the way the region has evolved, the wines, however enjoyable, make a little less sense. And without those wines, of course, the name of Bordeaux would never have become famous across the planet.

The geography is crucial. From a global perspective, Bordeaux lies almost precisely between the North Pole and the Equator, a little to the south of the 45th parallel – just like Halifax, Novia Scotia. Unlike that city on the other side of the Atlantic, however, it benefits from the shelter of its forests and the warmth of the Gulf Stream, which together help to make this northerly spot an unusually comfortable place to live. At the heart of the region, and its very *raison d'être*, is the Gironde, a major estuary whose name is derived from "*hirondelle*", the French term for the swallow. Leading into the

Gironde are a pair of rivers, and it is on the banks of one of these, the Garonne, some 100 kilometres inland, that the city of Bordeaux itself is to be found.

The climate that suits humans has also proved to be good for grapevines, fussy plants which also happen to appreciate the particular types of soil that were washed here 69 million years ago when the Pyrenees burst upward from the ocean. There are, however, other parts of France with pleasant weather and vine-friendly soil. With the exception of Champagne, whose weather is often far from pleasant, none is quite as famous as Bordeaux.

First on the list of godfathers who helped Bordeaux to gain its fame was a tribe called the Bituriges – the self-styled kings (*riges*) of the world (*bitu*), who moved southward from Bourges in the fifth century BCE. The Garonne was the Bronze Age equivalent of the Suez Canal: a link between the Atlantic and the Mediterranean – the north and south of the then known world. Instead of sailing around the coast of Spain, boats could follow the river south-eastward, almost as far as Toulouse, whence, after a short passage overland, they would travel along the Aude to the coast. All the Bituriges had to do was extract tolls from anyone using the river. With the help of the Romans, the town

N

km 0 · 5 · 10 · 15 · 20 · 25
miles 0 · 5 · 10 · 15

KEY TO AREAS MAPPED ELSEWHERE IN THIS BOOK

☐ THE MÉDOC (see p.33)

☐ PESSAC-LÉOGNAN, GRAVES, SAUTERNES AND BARSAC (see p.55)

☐ ENTRE-DEUX-MERS (see p.85)

☐ ST ÉMILION, POMEROL, SATELLITES, BOURG AND BLAYE (see p.99)

ATLANTIC OCEAN

Gironde

MÉDOC

HAUT-MÉDOC

LESPARRE-MÉDOC

ST ESTÈPHE

PAUILLAC

ST JULIEN

BLAYE

Étang d'Hourtin

Étang de Carcans

Étang de Lacanau

LISTRAC-MÉDOC

MOULIS-EN-MÉDOC

MARGAUX

BOURG

LALANDE DE POMEROL

FRONSAC

POMEROL

LIBOURNE

ST ÉMILION

Dordogne

CASTILLON-LA-BATAILLE

BORDEAUX

PESSAC-LÉOGNAN

ENTRE-DEUX-MERS

PREMIÈRES CÔTES DE BORDEAUX

GRAVES

Garonne

CADILLAC

BARSAC

ARCACHON

LANGON

SAUTERNES

13

then known as Burdigala became an artistic, cultural and commercial hub.

As they did in their other colonies, the Romans tried to save the cost of shipping wine from Italy by producing it locally. The vine that grew best was a variety imported from Albania and origi-

nally called the Balisca, but then proudly renamed the Biturica by the Bituriges. The place where this ancestor of the Cabernet Franc and Cabernet Sauvignon first proved to be fruitful was on the slopes of St Émilion, on the other side of the Garonne's sibling river, the Dordogne. The wine's praises were sung in the fourth century CE by a poet called Ausonius who was also governor of Gaul and tutor to Emperor Gratian. The tiny vineyard of Château Ausone is convincingly said to have been planted on the site of his villa.

This early success helped the nearby river port of Libourne to become a rival to Bordeaux, a precursor to the rivalry between the "right bank" wines of St Émilion and Pomerol and the "left bank" of the Médoc and Graves. The marriage of Eleanor of Aquitaine to Henry

II of England in 1152 brought Bordeaux under foreign rule, and Henry's successor Richard Coeur de Lion established his base here four decades later. Bordeaux's wines now enjoyed the high-tech boom of their day. When another English monarch, Edward II, married in London in 1307, the guests consumed the equivalent of more than a million bottles of wine, which left around 48,000,000 bottles to keep the Court and populace going for the rest of the year: six each for every man, woman and child.

While other outsiders – principally Dutch, Irish, English and German merchants – were instrumental in building Bordeaux's exports, it was an enterprising Frenchman by the name of Arnaud de Pontac who, in the mid 1600s, made Château Haut-Brion into the world's first branded wine by marketing it in England where it caught the attention of the diarist Samuel Pepys. The success of that wine from the Graves, to the south of Bordeaux, helped to encourage the development of estates such as Lafite and Margaux

14

in the Médoc, to the north. These vineyards were the exception to a regional rule, however; they were planted on gravelly outcrops surrounded by marshland — *le palus* — on which little could be grown. There were no roads; wine had to be transported by water, usually through river-harbours such as the ones at Margaux, St Julien, St Estèphe and, above all, Pauillac — all of which would one day become known for their wines.

In the 17th century, encouraged by the success of the first Médoc estates, a team of Dutchmen set about draining the marshes, installing the ditches — *les jalles* — that still separate the various winemaking communes. Their efforts were followed by such a *fureur de planter* ("planting frenzy"), and such an orgy of wine drinking, that in 1725 a royal edict was issued to ban any more vines going into the ground. But it was too late: the

Médoc was established, alongside the Graves, St Émilion and Fronsac, as a place to produce red wine.

Good white wine was being produced too, as the young US diplomat Thomas Jefferson discovered in 1787 on a visit to "Grave" and "Sauterne" where he bought 10 dozen bottles of wine from Château d'Yquem for himself and a further 30 dozen for George Washington. Traditionally, white Bordeaux would have been dry, but the enthusiasm of Dutch wine drinkers for late-harvest wine helped to create markets for Sauternes, Barsac, Cadillac and Ste Croix du Mont.

While there were unfortunate exceptions, such as the owner of Château Lafite who was executed, and the grand Château Trompette in Bordeaux which was torn to the ground, the Revolution created surprisingly few casualties. The Revolutionaries' greatest quarry, the clergy, were far less involved in winemaking in

15

THE ENTRANCE TO THE WINEMAKING *"CHAI"* OF CHÂTEAU MARGAUX (OPPOSITE), WHICH IS RARELY SEEN BY TOURISTS.
EVEN PROFESSIONAL VISITORS ARE OFTEN UNAWARE THAT THE CHÂTEAU MAKES AND REPAIRS ITS OWN BARRELS (ABOVE).

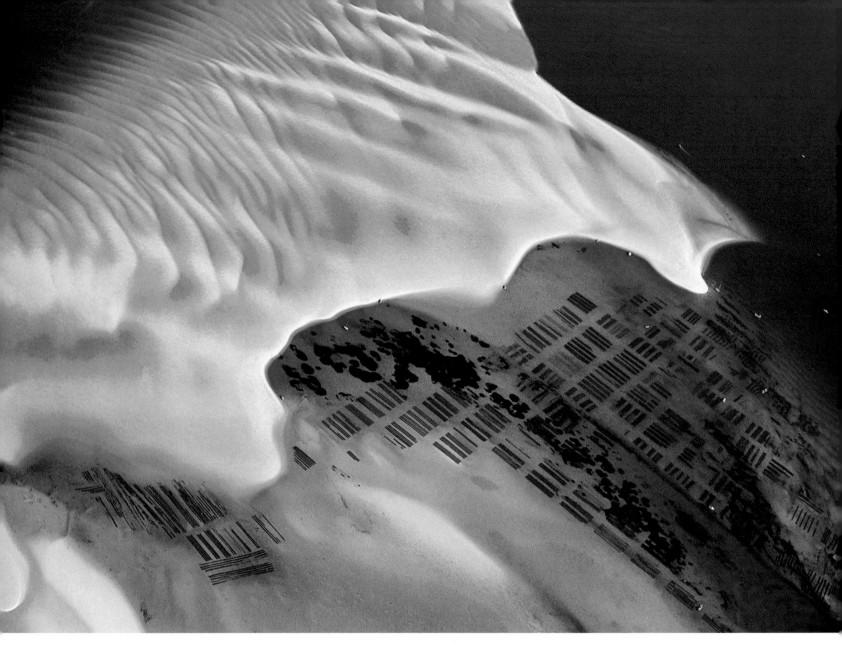

BORDEAUX MAY BE FAMOUS FOR ITS WINES, BUT IT SHOULD ALSO BE KNOWN FOR THE QUALITY OF ITS SEAFOOD, SUCH AS THE OYSTERS THAT ARE BRED IN VAST BEDS AT ARCACHON, WHICH IS ALSO THE FAVOURITE SEASIDE RESORT OF THE BORDELAIS.

Bordeaux than in Burgundy, and few of the château owners were sufficiently aristocratic to warrant removal.

At that time, the business of Bordeaux was in the hands of brokers and merchants who traded in wine in much the same way their counterparts today might buy and sell pork bellies. Vintages were bought as "futures" — to use the modern term — while the grapes were still on the vine, if not years in advance. To establish a little order into this process and to decide which were the "blue chip" estates, the traders used to draw up unofficial tables based on the prices at which their wines were sold. In 1855, the clock stopped and one such table, which divided the best wines of the Médoc (plus Haut-Brion in the Graves) into five levels of quality, was declared at the Great Exhibition to be *the* classification. And so, apart from the promotion of Château Mouton-Rothschild from second to first growth, it has ludicrously remained.

Sauternes, which was — equally ludicrously — accorded more than twice as many first growths as the Médoc and Graves combined, was also classified in 1855, but Bordeaux's other regions remained unclassified. This was remedied over the years in an almost wilfully uncoordinated way that combines with the vagaries of the *appellation d'origine contrôlée* system to leave wine drinkers thoroughly confused. St Émilion, for example, has two entirely separate sets of wines that can legally be described as Grands Crus.

This mess suited one part of Bordeaux perfectly. Pomerol, which was traditionally regarded as an extension of St Émilion, never had any kind of classification at all. In the first half of the 20th century, however, Belgian merchants and wine drinkers began to take an interest in wines such as Vieux-Château-Certan and Pétrus. Then, as the quality of wines rose, thanks partly to the efforts of the local *négociant* Jean-Pierre Moueix and of the winemaking consultant Michel Rolland, Pomerol's deliciously rich, fruitcakey Merlots developed a keen following in America. Crucially, the new fans were happy to buy wines from small ungraded estates; instead of being guided by classifications, they relied on advice from wine merchants, and critics such as Robert Parker. The international success of these wines helped to launch the latest phase in the evolution of Bordeaux. Today, for the first time for nearly two centuries, significant numbers of entirely new châteaux, such as Le Pin, Valandraud and Marojallia, are being created throughout the region. It is too early to say whether these wines really have what it takes to become enduring monarchs of the modern wine world, but the Bituriges of two millennia ago would certainly have admired the ambition that lies behind them.

CHAPTER ONE

THE CITY OF BORDEAUX

Despite the emergence of fine wine in many countries over the last century, the city of Bordeaux still retains its role as the Mecca of the wine world. Wines have been traded and shipped from the riverside here for more than two millennia, and every year this is still the place where merchants and critics have to come to sample and assess the latest vintage. All too often, though, in their haste to taste, these visitors miss the living history that is to be discovered around almost every corner of this fascinating and still-evolving city.

TASTET ET LAWTON (ABOVE) IS THE OLDEST FIRM OF *COURTIERS* — WINE BROKERS — IN BORDEAUX. THE PONT DE PIERRE IN THE HEART OF THE CITY (OPPOSITE) PROVIDES THE ESSENTIAL LINK BETWEEN BORDEAUX AND ST ÉMILION AND POMEROL.

Eight hundred years ago, Bordeaux was known as *le Port de la Lune* — the town whose river shared a sickle-like curve with the waning moon. Victor Hugo, looking at the mass of boats bobbing before the more aristocratic buildings of the quayside, saw a mixture of Versailles and Antwerp. I've always thought the city looks the way Paris would if Englishmen had had a greater say in the matter; the Bordelais don't mind being thought well-to-do, but they have a rather English distrust of gold leaf and ornamentation.

In fact, Bordeaux owes much of what, in wine terminology, might be called its austerity and its elegance to *les intendants* — the 17th- and 18th-century representatives of the French crown. In their desire to impose order, they replaced a "muddle of ugly houses" with a neat network of streets, broad avenues — the *cours* — and grand architectural gestures, such as the impeccably proportioned Place de la Bourse and Place du Parlement.

Fortunately, an enclave of *le vieux Bordeaux* survived, much as the Marais did in Paris, and this, within a pedestrian precinct, is where you find the ornate 15th-century Grosse Cloche that was once a gate to the city, and the extraordinary little church of St Éloi which is built into its side. Look up and you will see that, more than 600 years after the English were sent packing, one of their medieval emblems, the leopard, still leaps over the tower.

The Romans left fewer traces of their presence because, despite a protective wall more than two kilometres long and 10 metres high, the "miniature Rome" they built was almost completely destroyed by a succession of Vandals, Visigoths, Moors, Carolingians and Normans. So, little remains of the Palacium Galiena, an amphitheatre that could hold 15,000 of the 25,000 inhabitants and was named after the Emperor Gallien who was assassinated in 268CE. The arched ruins have little power over modern

21

THIS CARVED FACE OF NEPTUNE ABOVE A DOORWAY AT NUMBER 24 ALLÉES DE TOURNY (OPPOSITE) REFLECTS THE CITY'S MARITIME HISTORY AND IS ONE OF MANY SUCH CARVINGS THAT ARE TO BE SEEN THROUGHOUT BORDEAUX. FIVE CENTURIES AGO, THE GROSSE CLOCHE (ABOVE) WAS THE ENTRANCE TO WHAT WAS THEN A WALLED CITY.

emotions — unlike the intense, bearded and lifelike Roman bronze of Hercules who lays down a personal challenge to visitors to the city's Musée d'Aquitaine.

The demolished Roman temples, colonnades and forums are not the only architectural ghosts in Bordeaux. At the bend of the river, there was once an immense fortress called the Château Trompette, built by Louis XIV to symbolize the might of monarchy and to intimidate the populace following a rebellion in 1675. A little more than a century later, a rather larger revolt in Paris wrested power from another Louis and the symbolic château was symbolically torn to the ground. The 12 hectares of empty space this created were less than convincingly filled in 1818 by the Esplanade des Quinconces, one of the biggest open squares in Europe. Its name — derived from the Latin *quincunx* — refers to the pattern of planting squares of trees with five on each side, but sadly this horticultural conceit is less easy to appreciate now that much of the area has been dedicated to the mighty motor car.

THE ELEGANT — AND USUALLY BUSY — PLACE DU PARLEMENT (OPPOSITE). THE RUINS OF THE ROMAN PALACIUM GALIENA AMPHITHEATRE (ABOVE), WHICH COULD ONCE ACCOMMODATE THREE-FIFTHS OF THE POPULATION OF BORDEAUX.

At one end of the Esplanade, overlooking the water, there is a pair of columns decorated with carved anchors, stars and ships' prows and topped by bronze figures that must have been a welcome sight to the crews of sailing ships returning from voyages across the Atlantic. But the landmark sought through their spyglasses was the church of St Michel a touch closer to the mouth of the river. Its spire, pierced by stone port-holes, stands 148 metres high and is surrounded by a set of smaller spires, once known in the local vernacular as *los filholes deu cloquey* – the "young girls of the clock tower". When a lookout first spotted the cross on the top spire, it was said that the mariners were happy; when he could see the girls – *los filholes* – they knew they had passed the hazards of the estuary and were safely home.

Back at the other end of the Esplanade, stands the Monument aux Girondins. This winged Liberty casting off her chains at the summit of a stone column, was likened by a local wag to a paperweight on a candlestick, and it is easy to see what he meant. At the foot of the column lie a set of fountains and a collection of bronze

THE WONDERFUL STAIRCASE OF L'INTENDANT WINE SHOP (LEFT). THE FOUNTAINS OF THE MONUMENT AUX GIRONDINS (OPPOSITE), COMMEMORATING THE DISSIDENT BORDELAIS VICTIMS OF THE FRENCH REVOLUTION.

THE INTERIOR OF THE GRAND THÉÂTRE (OPPOSITE), ONE OF THE MOST BEAUTIFUL AUDITORIA IN FRANCE. A RARE
CLOSE-UP VIEW OF THE FIGURES ON THE ROOF OF THE THEATRE (ABOVE), WITH THE WINGED FIGURE OF LIBERTY
ON TOP OF THE MONUMENT AUX GIRONDINS IN THE BACKGROUND.

humans and rearing horses that contrive not only to represent Liberty, Equality and Fraternity, but also Order, Work, Commerce, Industry, the Sciences, the Arts, Peace, Virtue and Happiness and the Triumphs of Concord and the Republic. The monument owes its name to the Girondin party that enjoyed a brief moment of national power after the Revolution. In October 1793, however, 22 leading Girondins paid for their opposition to the blood-lust of those heady days, with a trip to the scaffold. The fountains, which are at their best lit by floodlights and the moon, are now a symbol of the city, but, for nearly 40 years after World War Two, they were absent – having been stolen by the German occupying forces who used them to make guns. The inauguration of the replicas was one of the more moving moments in the recent history of the city.

Facing the south of the fountain, and close to the narrow, wedge-shaped Maison du Vin, is Bordeaux's most impressive piece of architecture, and one of the most beautiful classical theatres in France. Designed by

28

Victor Louis in the late 1700s, and restored recently, the Grand Théâtre is fronted by a colonnade on which stand 12 magnificent be-toga'd figures which – back to the discretion of the Bordelais – really need to be seen through binoculars. Within the building, there is some uncharacteristic exuberance in the shape of the gilding and decoration at the head of the palatial staircase, in the auditorium and in a great room in which appropriately grand tastings and dinners are held.

The merchants – *négociants* – who host these events traditionally worked and lived a little further downriver, on and around the Quai des Chartrons – Charterhouse Quay – which was named after the Carthusian monks who took refuge in this area, just outside the city walls,

Left to right: the interior of La Tupina restaurant, a favourite haunt for Bordeaux producers and visitors; an old grocery shop on the street named after the Roman poet Ausonius; the flea market close to the Église St Michel, where goods from throughout the world are sold alongside local antiques; a traditional door knocker that would gain admission to a *négociant*'s offices.

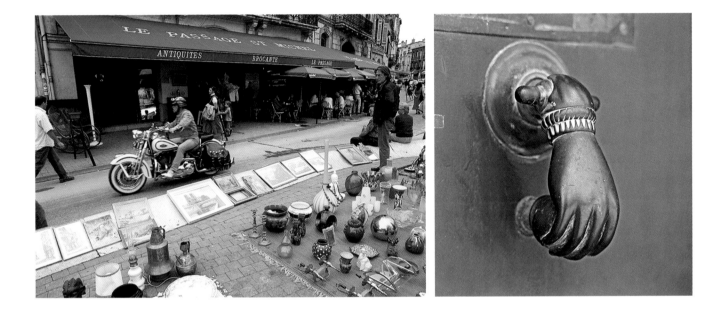

during the Hundred Years' War. The *négociants* who followed in their wake were also refugees of a sort — traders, often from other countries, prevented by the protective rules of Bordeaux from doing business in the city. Over the centuries, the imposing stone buildings of the Quai became the heart of the wine trade. This was where the Chartronnais, the "aristocrats of the cork", struck the deals that would fill the hundreds of horse-driven carts and the sailing ships that, as recently as a century ago, daily lined up at the water's edge. Most of the *négociants* have moved their offices and warehouses to settings that are more conducive to business in the

21st century, but a few still lurk behind wooden doors with discreet brass plates, and all still trade on *la Place de Bordeaux* where prices are set each day for wine of every vintage and château. Visitors to Bordeaux who have heard of *la Place* scour their city maps for it, but they do so in vain, for the simple reason that it has never existed physically. Having been born in the gentlemen's clubs of the city more than two centuries ago, it was the precursor of that most 21st-century phenomenon, a virtual trading floor that now exists in the form of telephone calls, faxes and e-mails. Bordeaux, as I say, takes many forms.

CHAPTER TWO

THE MÉDOC

Some of the most exquisite Bordeaux of all are undeniably produced in St Émilion,

Pomerol and Pessac-Léognan, but none of these regions can begin to compete with the

number of top châteaux that are to be found in the Médoc. If this part of Bordeaux were

a film, it would be the kind of epic that features cameo roles by an array of the biggest

stars of the silver screen. But the Médoc has much more to offer than starry names. There

are plenty of less well known wines to discover — and less well known villages and towns.

Ripe Cabernet Sauvignon grapes glistening with morning dew at Château Meyney in St Estèphe (above). The
patchwork of Cabernet Sauvignon, Cabernet Franc and Merlot vines in St Julien and Pauillac (opposite).

CLOCKWISE FROM TOP LEFT: CHÂTEAU LANESSAN, SOURCE OF GOOD TRADITIONAL, FAIRLY PRICED WINE; LANGOA-BARTON, HOME OF THE WINES OF BOTH LANGOA-BARTON AND THE MORE ILLUSTRIOUS LÉOVILLE-BARTON; PICHON-LONGUEVILLE-BARON, A CLASSICALLY BEAUTIFUL CHÂTEAU WHOSE WINES ARE NOW ENJOYING A RENAISSANCE; LAFITE, OVERLOOKING ITS HERB GARDENS AND ORNAMENTAL POND — AND STANDING AS ONE OF THE NORTHERNMOST SENTINELS OF PAUILLAC.

To drive along the D2 *route des vins* is to travel through a three-dimensional wine list. For anyone with more than a passing interest in wine, the experience of actually seeing châteaux such as Margaux and Latour has to arouse the tingle of excitement film buffs feel in Hollywood. For some, though, there may also be a twinge of disappointment. The Médoc's quiet towns, woodland and sometimes barely perceptibly sloping vineyards provide a surprisingly plain setting for those buildings. But, like its wines, which initially can seem tough and forbidding, the Médoc demands and rewards patience – and the readiness to look beyond the obvious, and into the past.

This triangular wedge of land owes its name to a Celtic tribe called the Meduli. For much of its history, however, the Médoc was treated simply as the northern part of the Graves, an area which surrounded and continued south from the city of Bordeaux. Until the 17th century there was, in any case, little reason to refer to the region at all; it was a miserable place, covered by forest, sodden marshland and 50,000 hectares of constantly shifting dunes which made their sandy presence felt against the walls of Bordeaux itself and, in 1744, even invaded and occupied the church of Soulac on the west coast. There were lakes whose shapes constantly altered, depending on the intensity of the

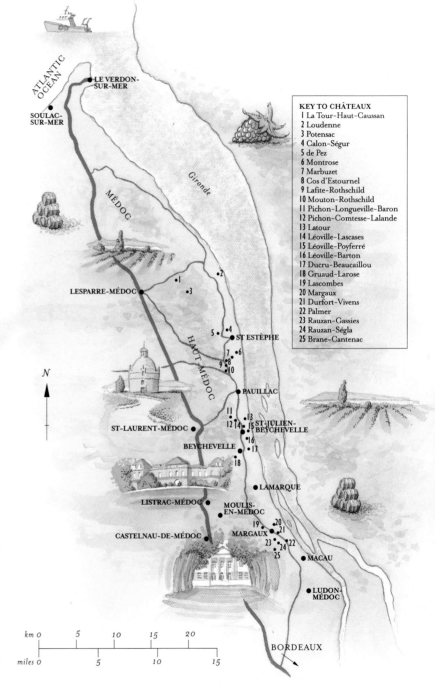

KEY TO CHÂTEAUX
1 La Tour-Haut-Caussan
2 Loudenne
3 Potensac
4 Calon-Ségur
5 de Pez
6 Montrose
7 Marbuzet
8 Cos d'Estournel
9 Lafite-Rothschild
10 Mouton-Rothschild
11 Pichon-Longueville-Baron
12 Pichon-Comtesse-Lalande
13 Latour
14 Léoville-Lascases
15 Léoville-Poyferré
16 Léoville-Barton
17 Ducru-Beaucaillou
18 Gruaud-Larose
19 Lascombes
20 Margaux
21 Durfort-Vivens
22 Palmer
23 Rauzan-Gassies
24 Rauzan-Ségla
25 Brane-Cantenac

winter rains and the rate of evaporation in the summer months, and rare *isles* – small, gravel-covered outcrops of clay, silt and sand, which survived from one year to the next. The inhabitants of the Médoc mostly scratched a miserable feudal living in small hamlets protected from the swamp by man-made ditches, and relied on the Gironde for much of their transport. The 13th-century St Estèphe estate of Calon-Ségur was probably named after the *calones* – boats on which timber was ferried across the Gironde. These and other river craft were as essential to the Médocains as the railway was to settlers in America, and the 16th-century Phare de Cordouan lighthouse marking the mouth of the river at the northern tip of the Médoc had some of the cathedral-like qualities of a major railway station. Personally planned by Henri IV, it is an ornate building containing a chapel in which there is an inscription to "*Un Dieu, une Foy, une Loy*" – one God, one Faith, one Law.

The river was, however, not without a variety of tidal and other hazards. The original tower at La Tor, the 14th-century fortress that would become Château Latour, was a lookout for pirates, such as a certain Blanquet whose capture in 1617 was widely celebrated.

Until 1770, the Gironde was essentially uncharted; navigation was by soundings and by the occasional landmarks to be seen on either bank. Even in 1787, river pilots were still calling for buoys to mark the numerous wrecks. Villages and towns, including the four main wine *appellations* – St Estèphe, Pauillac, St Julien and Margaux – were founded in places where boats could safely load their goods. Of these, Pauillac, which offered a natural, deep-water harbour, became the most important; Margaux's port, by contrast, silted up and became too shallow.

Grapes would have been grown among other crops, but there were some estates with serious vineyards. Wine was made close to Château Beaumont in the 10th century and, according to local legend, Château d'Issan in Margaux produced both the wine that was drunk at the wedding of the English king Henry II and Eleanor of Aquitaine in 1152 at the beginning of the English occupation, and the wine that was carried home by the defeated English army 302 years later. Châteaux Giscours and Chasse-Spleen were both active as wine estates in the mid 1500s and, in 1575, Cantemerle produced three *tonneaux* – the equivalent of 3,000 cases,

THE AUTUMNAL HUES OF ST JULIEN (OPPOSITE), VIEWED FROM CHÂTEAU LÉOVILLE-POYFERRÉ. THE SOIL HERE MAKES FOR BLACKCURRANTY, CEDARY FLAVOURS THAT SET THIS *APPELLATION* APART FROM ITS NEIGHBOURS MARGAUX AND PAUILLAC.

roughly as much as a small Pomerol estate today. All of these vineyards were sited above the marsh on the gravelly outcrops left by the rising seas 12,000 years ago. Various local terms for these – *fite*, *brion*, *tertre* and *caux* or *cos* – have given their names to châteaux such as Lafite, Haut-Brion, du Tertre and Cos d'Estournel. Even Mouton-Rothschild is thought to owe its name to the *motte* on which it is situated, rather than to the *moutons* – sheep – that wintered in Pauillac in later years.

Wine-producing estates were, however, the exception. Few of the aristocratic owners – the *noblesse d'épée*, the nobles of the sword – could afford to develop vineyards, there was little worthwhile land on offer and, perhaps most importantly, no one saw much point in growing grapes. Over the 17th century, the picture was changed by the efforts of a small group of highly skilled technicians: the Dutch *déssicateurs* – drainage engineers – contracted by an Englishman named

Humphrey Bradley who had been given the valuable concession by Henri IV to recover marshland throughout France. The importance of the *jalles* (drainage ditches), which are still in use after 400 years, is illustrated by the fact that one of the first tasks undertaken by the new owners of Château Margaux in the late 1970s was to drain and restore them. If the arrival of the *déssicateurs* altered the landscape of the Médoc, it also helped to lay the foundations for the modern Bordeaux wine trade. The drainage costs were covered either by the Dutchmen themselves or by merchants and entrepreneurial Bordeaux lawyers and parliamentarians (the *noblesse de robe*), who, like the pioneers of the Napa Valley in California three and a half centuries later, were ready to risk their capital on a new venture.

Among these were Pierre de Lestonnac, who in the 1570s established Château Margaux, and the father-and-son team of Arnaud and Denis de Mullet who,

37

CONTRASTING IMAGES: THE LITTLE CHURCH IN THE SLEEPY VILLAGE OF MOULIS-EN-MÉDOC (OPPOSITE), WHICH IS WORTH VISITING FOR ITS CARVED STONE CAPITALS; THE PROUD, GILDED STAR (ABOVE) AT CHÂTEAU MOUTON-ROTHSCHILD, THE ONLY ESTATE TO RISE FROM SECOND TO FIRST GROWTH SINCE THE HIERARCHY OF THE MÉDOC WAS ESTABLISHED IN 1855.

soon after, were responsible for assembling the set of vineyards we now know as Château Latour. In 1638, their neighbour, a merchant called Moytié, put together the estate that would, a century later, take on the name of its owner, Monsieur Léoville. A few decades later, Pierre de Rauzan, the manager of Château Latour, gave his sons vineyards close to Château Margaux that are now known as châteaux Rauzan-Ségla and Rauzan-Gassies; Thérèse, his daughter, received the land that would – bearing the name of her husband, Jacques de Pichon – become châteaux Pichon-Longueville-Baron and Pichon-Comtesse-Lalande. So, by the end of the 17th century, many of the top châteaux of the Médoc were open for business – or soon would be.

Arnaud de Pontac, the famous creator of Château Haut-Brion (see pp.57–8) in the Graves, made his mark in the Médoc by producing a blend he called "Pontac" from what is now Château de Pez in St Estèphe and from vineyards closer to Bordeaux. Operating like a modern-day entrepreneur, he not only invented the world's first commercial branded wine, but he also mastered its distribution. In 1666, as London was being rebuilt following the devastation of the Great Fire, he sent his son François-Auguste to establish what was probably the city's first restaurant at a tavern called "Pontack's Head" close to the Old Bailey. By 1677 Pontac was included among the "best wine at Bordeaux" by the English philosopher John Locke who bemoaned the "folly" of the English that had caused its price to double. Three centuries later, similar folly would have the same effect on highly praised new wines such as Château Le Pin in Pomerol and Screaming Eagle in the Napa Valley.

Next in the series of the founding fathers of the Médoc was a master of the art of marrying well called

THE *JALLE* – DRAINAGE DITCH – AT CHÂTEAU BEYCHEVELLE WHICH CARRIES EXCESS WATER TO THE RIVER. *JALLES* LIKE THESE ABOUND IN THE MÉDOC; UNTIL THEY WERE DUG BY DUTCH ENGINEERS, MOST OF THIS REGION WAS A SWAMP.

Nicolas-Alexandre, Marquis de Ségur. His grandmother's dowry had brought Château Lafite, Château Latour came from his mother's family and his own marriage won him the property closest to his heart, Calon-Ségur. His nickname, "Prince of Vines", was supposedly coined by Louis XV when de Ségur revealed that his diamond-like waistcoat buttons were made of polished quartz pebbles from his vineyard. He knew those vineyards well enough to discern a significant difference between the soils of Lafite and those adjoining them that now produce Mouton-Rothschild. He sold the latter land to Baron Joseph de Brane, whose 19th-century successor, Hector, the "Napoleon of the Vines", turned what was then called Brane-Mouton into a rival for Lafite, Latour and Margaux. De Ségur died in 1755 as one of the wealthiest men in France. Less than three decades later, his profligate grandson, Nicolas-Marie-Alexandre had to flee the country and sell Lafite to escape his creditors. In 1786, the château passed into the hands of a leading politician called Pichard, who was able to enjoy its possession for just six years before he went to the guillotine in the French Revolution.

There were other high-profile casualties, such as Château Margaux, which was sequestrated by the state, but the Revolutionaries had less quarrel with the minor aristocrats and merchants of the Médoc than with the churchmen who controlled Burgundy. So, while that region's vineyards were distributed among the peasants, the châteaux were either sold to wealthy bidders or, in the case of estates such as Lynch-Bages and Léoville-Barton which belonged to merchants of foreign stock, they were left in the hands of their existing owners. As these and other Médoc estates competed for business and prestige, the brokers of Bordeaux who sold their wines used, like stockbrokers, to draw up unofficial lists that tracked their status in relation to each other. In 1855 one such list was cast in stone when the worthies of the region were asked by the organizers of the Paris *Exposition Universelle* (Great Exhibition) for a "complete and satisfactory" hierarchy of the region's wines. After much deliberation and some blind tasting of wines from throughout Bordeaux, they obliged with classifications for the Médoc and Sauternes (plus Haut-Brion, the most famous Graves château, whose omission would have been unimaginable). The only alteration to the 1855 Classification was the promotion in 1973, after much lobbying by its owner, of Château Mouton-Rothschild from second to first growth. (See also pp.130–31.)

Once the Médoc recovered from the setbacks of the phylloxera louse, which forced the owners to replant their vines in the late 19th century, the Great

39

THE TOWER OF CHÂTEAU LATOUR (ABOVE), WHERE THERE WAS ONCE A LOOKOUT FOR PIRATES. THE VINES OF CHÂTEAU MEYNEY (OPPOSITE) RUN DOWN ALMOST TO THE RIVERBANK.

40

Depression of the 1930s, and two World Wars, it entered its finest age with the great 1945, 1947 and 1949 vintages. The new era brought new ways of doing things. Led by the brilliant, mercurial Philippe de Rothschild, the estates began to bottle their own wines rather than entrust this task to merchants in France or overseas. The great Professor Emile Peynaud also helped subsequently, as a consultant and teacher, to create a qualitative revolution, by focusing attention on hygiene and on the importance of omitting lesser-quality barrels from the "Grand Vin" that would be sold under the name of the château. Over the last quarter of the 20th century, so-called "second wines", produced from the casks that just failed to make the grade, became increasingly common. Some, such as Les Forts de Latour, Pavillon Rouge du Château Margaux and Château Léoville-Lascases' Clos-du-Marquis, like "second"-quality clothes from top couturiers, proved to be as good or better than the supposedly top-flight efforts from lesser producers.

The "over-performers" were helped significantly by American critics such as Robert Parker who preferred to judge a château on the basis of how the wine actually tasted rather than paying attention to dusty old class systems. By the end of the millennium, even conservative French publications finally began to refer to the châteaux of the Médoc without troubling to reveal their status in 1855. Among the beneficiaries of this open-minded attitude are the best châteaux of the *appellation* simply known as the Médoc in the northern half of the estuary. Nearly three million cases of red wine are produced here each year, a third of it by a

handful of cooperatives. Most is ordinary, weedy stuff, but wines from châteaux such as La Tour-Haut-Caussan, Loudenne and Potensac stand comparison with estates in the supposedly "finer" *appellations* further south. Their wines offer everything you want from the Médoc: blackcurrant fruit with just a hint of green pepper; richness but with a backbone of tannin that will allow the wine to last; and just enough of the mineral character of the soil to set them apart from the "jamminess" of many varietal wines from other regions.

Moving into the Haut-Médoc – "Upper Médoc" – we get to St Estèphe, the northernmost of the major communes. Like its tall-spired church and indeed the rest of the village, the wines here have a recognizable rugged character that seems built to stand

all weathers. There are more – slight – hills than in much of the rest of the Médoc, and it is on the slopes of these and close to the banks of the Gironde that the best estates, such as de Pez, Les Ormes-de-Pez, Phélan-Ségur, Montrose, Lafon-Rochet and Calon-Ségur, are to be found. Château Montrose, whose vines were planted in 1820, is a great example of the old *médocain* saying that the finest wines come from vineyards that can see the river. Modern winemaking has helped to produce more accessible St Estèphe than in the past, but the clay in the soil means that young examples of top estates in all but the warmest vintages tend to be just a little more forbidding than examples from Pauillac, a few kilometres further south. Haut-Marbuzet is an exception to this rule, as is Cos d'Estournel, the last château you pass on the way out of the *appellation*. This is a château like no other, boasting a glorious mock-oriental façade, complete with pagodas and arches, created by the owner Louis Gaspard d'Estournel in the early 1800s on his return from travels in the East. It may be a little fanciful to go looking

41

for spices in Cos d'Estournel, but its wines are certainly the most luscious and rich in St Estèphe.

Between Cos d'Estournel and the pointed slate turret, pond and kitchen garden of Lafite, the road passes over a reminder of the efforts of the *déssicateurs*: the Chenal du Lazaret is a lush, low-lying hollow that, until the digging of a *jalle*, would have been a lake. Pauillac is the longest-established town in the Médoc and by far the most significant. Considering the prices commanded by its top wines, it feels surprisingly like an Atlantic fishing town-cum-seaside resort. The welcome lack of airs and graces apparent here and in the other towns of the Médoc is easily explained. Historically this was a region of absentee landlords who thought of their châteaux in much the same way as London businessmen considering tea plantations in Kenya. Today, the owners are often companies or business magnates based in Paris who have benefited from sales forced by draconian death duties and inheritance laws. Inconveniently for those who mourn this handover from families to financial institutions, such a transfer usually brings a rapid improvement in the quality of the wine and the upkeep of the buildings. When I visited Château Pichon-Longueville-Baron in 1988, shortly after its purchase by

The pagoda tower and the carved door of Château Cos d'Estournel, a folly that produces great wine.

FAMOUS FOR ITS WINE AND LAMB, PAUILLAC IS STILL A SMALL
RIVERSIDE TOWN WITH A TRADITION OF FINE SEAFOOD.

the insurance company AXA, one of the prettiest and
most photographed châteaux in the Médoc proved to be
a hollow shell that had been unoccupied for well over a
generation. On the walls of one upstairs room, there
was still graffiti scrawled by German soldiers during
World War Two.

Now, that completely refurbished château and its
striking new winery are once again producing Pauillacs
that challenge the efforts of Pichon-Comtesse-Lalande
on the other side of the road, which in turn continues
to snap at the heels of its next-door neighbour Château
Latour. Pauillac is like that: a paradise for Bordeaux
name-droppers, with a plethora of top-quality châteaux
– such as Grand-Puy-Lacoste, Duhart-Milon, Batailley
and Haut-Batailley, Clerc-Milon, d'Armailhac, Pontet-
Canet and the supreme over-performer Lynch-Bages –
and very few poor ones. For value, I'd also recommend
Pibran, Fonbadet, Grand-Puy-Ducasse, Haut-Bages-
Libéral and Bernadotte.

Château Latour's other ambitious neighbour, and
the region's strongest contender for promotion from
second to first growth, stands on the other side of the
jalle that forms the frontier with St Julien. Château

Léoville-Lascases has neither tower nor its own château — when the original Léoville estate was split into three parts, Léoville-Lascases was left sharing a building with Léoville-Poyferré. What it does have is a huge stone archway that stands in solitary splendour overlooking its vines. But at least Léoville-Lascases has half a château; the third part of the original vineyard, Léoville-Barton, has none at all. Anyone wanting to taste its wines — always among the best of the vintage — has to do so at its sister estate, Langoa-Barton.

These châteaux are the exceptions to the rule in a commune that can lay claim to some of the best looking buildings in Bordeaux. Châteaux Ducru-Beaucaillou and Gruaud-Larose, sitting amid the flat backdrop of their vines, are both masterpieces of classical architecture. The name of the former château was originally "maucaillou", from the *mauvais* (bad) *cailloux* (stones) that were so unpopular with farmers trying to plant wheat. Success with vines led to the first syllable being changed to *beau* – beautiful. Until 1680, Ducru and its neighbour Branaire actually formed part of Château Beychevelle, which possesses arguably the most beautiful building and garden in St Julien. There are many explanations for how Beychevelle came by its name, but the most convincing is that the little port behind the château was a spot where sailing boats used to moor and lower their sails — "*baisser la voile*", or, in the local argot, "*bacha velo*". The 1964 Beychevelle was one of the wines that first turned me on to Bordeaux; sadly I find more recent efforts rather jammy, especially when compared to the gloriously fine, yet powerful wines of the Léovilles and Ducru-Beaucaillou, which combine the pure blackcurrant of Pauillac with a flavour English tasters traditionally identify as "cigar box".

Moulis-en-Médoc and Listrac-Médoc are usually treated as though they were a pair of siblings. But the two communes are quite different; they have separate soils and histories and make wines that can often be told apart far more easily than those of, say, St Julien and Pauillac. Older Bordelais flout political correctness by describing Moulis as being more "feminine" in style — softer, richer, more immediately charming; while Listrac is resolutely masculine — tougher, more sinewy and harder to get to know. The explanation for this difference lies in the soil. Listrac's vines sit on the slight slopes of the so-called "inverted Listrac dome" where there is a great deal of clay and limestone on which the Cabernet Sauvignon tends to ripen poorly. I remember, in the 1980s, the winemaker of Château Clarke offering me samples of wine made from each of the four grape varieties grown on the estate. The Merlot had a richness lacking in its peers.

Château Clarke's wine now has a higher proportion of Merlot and is probably the most approachable in Listrac, but Fourcas-Hosten, Fourcas-Dupré and Fonréaud (supposedly named after the *fontaine royale* — the royal spring discovered by a visiting king in the 11th century) are all recommendable. The soil in Moulis is less consistent but the well-drained gravelly slopes

of estates like Maucaillou, Poujeaux, and Chasse-Spleen all allow grapes to ripen and to develop the kind of attractively lush flavours that Byron thought capable of seeing off (*chasse*) bad moods (*spleen*).

A few years ago I was invited, along with a number of other tasters, to try to define the style and flavour of the wines of Margaux. The fact that we all thought such an initiative worthwhile says much about the southernmost major wine-producing commune in the Médoc. This is a large *appellation* with more than 80 estates which collectively produce some seven and a half million bottles of wine each year. They range from 21 classed growths to three dozen that fall beneath Cru Bourgeois on the quality scale and are scattered between the communes of Margaux itself, Labarde, Arsac and Cantenac. But there's also a matter of winemaking. Professor Peynaud once told me that "People say Margaux is naturally delicate and light, but that's because it's made to taste that way. There's no reason why it shouldn't be as powerful as Pauillac." The gloriously impressive wines produced by Château Margaux in the early 1980s, when Peynaud had a hand in the blending, eloquently prove his point, and there's no question that too many winemakers in Margaux pass off over-production in the name of "delicacy". Even so, I suspect that the apparently ideal gravel here is actually a little less forgiving than in the other major villages and that it is all too easy to make wines that seem either dilute or clumsy. Margaux seems to be a sauce that needs a particularly deft hand and careful

CABERNET SAUVIGNON VINES (ABOVE) GROWING IN THE GRAVELLY SOIL THAT IS SO CRUCIAL TO THE CHARACTER OF THE MÉDOC. DUCRU-BEAUCAILLOU (OPPOSITE), ONE OF THE MOST ELEGANT CHÂTEAUX AND WINES IN ST JULIEN.

48

LEFT TO RIGHT: RIPE MERLOT GRAPES IN MARGAUX, WAITING TO BE PICKED; HARVESTING IN THE BEST ESTATES IS STILL DONE BY HAND, ALTHOUGH LESSER CHÂTEAUX NOW USE MACHINES THAT SHAKE THE BUNCHES FROM THE VINES; SORTING THE GRAPES AS THEY ARRIVE IS CRUCIAL — ESPECIALLY IN YEARS WHEN RIPENING HAS BEEN UNEVEN OR POOR WEATHER HAS CAUSED ROT; AFTER A BACK-BREAKING MORNING, HARVESTERS EAT A HEARTY LUNCH AT CHÂTEAU LANGOA-BARTON.

watching. Curiously, however, this is a commune that can sometimes — as it did famously in 1983 — collectively make better wines than its neighbours.

The château that best embodies my own ideal of Margaux is another over-achiever, the third growth Château Palmer, named after a General Charles Palmer who bought the attractive château from a similarly attractive widow. Palmer's wines, like those of other

Margaux estates such as Rauzan-Ségla and, when they are on form, Malescot St-Exupéry, Brane-Cantenac, Durfort-Vivens, Lascombes, Prieuré-Lichine, Giscours and d'Issan, and the reliable but lesser-ranked Labégorce, Labégorce-Zédé, Monbrison, La Gurgue and d'Angludet, couple the blackcurrant of the Cabernet grapes with blackberry — and a perfumed quality that is unequalled elsewhere.

Leaving the best to last, there is, of course, Château Margaux itself. This looks the way great wine estates should: grand and pillared, lying behind a pair of gates at the end of a long alley of trees, with its winemaking *chai* tucked away off a courtyard with walls that are painted in an ochre I would expect to find in Provence. Little has changed since Thomas Jefferson came to taste in 1785 and paid the "very dear" price of three livres per bottle for the 1784 vintage. He was not the only president to develop a taste for this château. Richard Nixon was said to have served it to the more important guests at official functions, while lesser mortals had to make do with Beaujolais. Like music-lovers comparing the works of Bach and Beethoven, wine buffs love to discuss the respective merits of wines such as the 1947 Cheval Blanc, 1945 Mouton-Rothschild and 1961 Lafite. All I can say is that I have never tasted any wine that bettered the fragrant and still youthful 1953 Margaux.

The fame of the *appellations* of St Estèphe, Pauillac, St Julien, Moulis and Listrac make it easy to forget that really good wines are produced beyond their borders and fall into the broader regional *appellation* of the Haut-Médoc. To the west of St Julien, there are châteaux Belgrave, Camensac, and La Tour-Carnet, while in the south close to Bordeaux are Cru Bourgeois châteaux such as the medieval fortified Lamarque, Beaumont,

Sociando-Mallet, La Tour-du-Haut-Moulin and the classified pair of La Lagune in Ludon and Cantemerle in Macau. Of the last pair, La Lagune has no lake, but does boast an attractive single-storey building and courtyard that are the perfect Bordelais marriage of grand house and farm. The wines are good too, and often under-priced. Cantemerle means "song of the blackbird" but might be a pun on the noise of the cannon (which was also nicknamed *merle*) used to protect the castle here during the Hundred Years' War. The tiny Port de Macau nearby offers one of the secrets of Bordeaux, which I discovered one day quite by accident: a pair of cafés selling cockles, whelks and sea snails and inexpensive white wine at tables overlooking the river. Every time I need a peaceful break between sampling grand wines in grand châteaux, this is where I come.

CHÂTEAU MARGAUX (OPPOSITE), THE MOST BEAUTIFUL AND MOST RECOGNIZABLE ESTATE IN BORDEAUX — AND STILL LOOKING MUCH THE WAY IT WOULD WHEN THOMAS JEFFERSON VISITED. THE CHÂTEAU MARGAUX BARREL HALL (ABOVE) — CONTAINING WINE WORTH 30 MILLION EUROS. ALTHOUGH IT REMAINS HERE UNTIL IT IS BOTTLED 18 MONTHS OR SO AFTER THE HARVEST, THE WINE IN THE BARRELS IS ALREADY THE PROPERTY OF MERCHANTS AND WINE LOVERS ACROSS THE PLANET.

CHAPTER THREE

GRAVES AND PESSAC-LÉOGNAN

52

Throughout the world, the soil in which vines are grown makes a crucial contribution to the flavour of the wine that is produced from their grapes. Nowhere is this more openly acknowledged, however, than in the Graves, the region that is actually named after the gravel that covers its finest vineyards. The home of the world's first branded wine, Château Haut-Brion, also still stands apart as the only area in Bordeaux where both red and white wines are made to a similarly high standard. But it is still under-appreciated ...

THE GRAVEL (ABOVE) THAT GIVES THE REGION ITS NAME — AND THE WINE ITS DISTINCTIVE CHARACTER. WHEN THIS BOTTLE (OPPOSITE) OF CHÂTEAU HAUT-BRION WAS PRODUCED IN 1848, THE ESTATE WAS ALREADY MORE THAN 400 YEARS OLD.

Separated from Château Haut-Brion by the width of a busy road, La Mission Haut-Brion is actually situated in a different commune and the soil of its vineyards produces recognizably different wine.

As someone with an instinctive dislike of pigeon-holes, I have always felt a curious kinship with the Graves: the bit of Bordeaux that's hardest to categorize, and, therefore, the most likely to be overlooked. This is the only part of Bordeaux that is serious about making both red and white wine and it does so in a range of subtly diverse styles that are hard to lump together.

Mind you, even the name provides something of a warning that the Graves is different. The Médoc commemorates an otherwise forgotten Celtic tribe and St Émilion is named after an eighth-century hermit, but there's no human connection here: the Graves is a wine region whose very identity stands as a reminder of the gravel – *les graves*, or in earlier times, *Grabas de Burdeus* – on which its vines are grown. Nowadays, while top estates such as Haut-Brion and Pape-Clément feature on the must-have lists of every wine collector, the Graves is often overshadowed by the grandeur of the Médoc on the one hand and the hedonism and the fireworks of St Émilion and Pomerol on the other. This is all the more ironic when one considers that this area surrounding and to the south of the city of Bordeaux is where the vinous reputation of the entire region was born. It is also the enduring heartland of dry white Bordeaux, a unique style of wine that – unlike the region's reds – still has no rival.

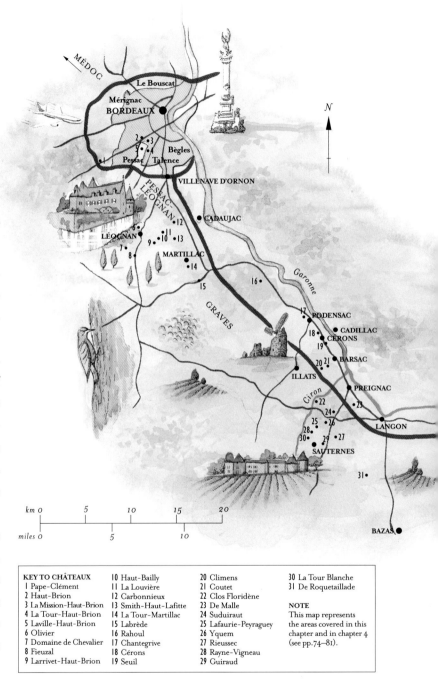

KEY TO CHÂTEAUX	10 Haut-Bailly	20 Climens	30 La Tour Blanche
1 Pape-Clément	11 La Louvière	21 Coutet	31 De Roquetaillade
2 Haut-Brion	12 Carbonnieux	22 Clos Floridène	
3 La Mission-Haut-Brion	13 Smith-Haut-Lafitte	23 De Malle	**NOTE**
4 La Tour-Haut-Brion	14 La Tour-Martillac	24 Suduiraut	This map represents
5 Laville-Haut-Brion	15 Labrède	25 Lafaurie-Peyraguey	the areas covered in this
6 Olivier	16 Rahoul	26 Yquem	chapter and in chapter 4
7 Domaine de Chevalier	17 Chantegrive	27 Rieussec	(see pp.74–81).
8 Fieuzal	18 Cérons	28 Rayne-Vigneau	
9 Larrivet-Haut-Brion	19 Seuil	29 Guiraud	

Grapes were grown for wine successfully here as early as the third century and, by the time a monk drew a map of the region 900 years later, he was able to depict vines in the lands of the Benedictine Abbey of Ste Croix and in a set of communes including Barrères, St Laurent d'Escures and St

56

Nicolas de Grave. There were also significant vineyards at Mérignac, the site today of Bordeaux's airport and the kind of discount stores that, like the detritus on a river bank, mark the outskirts of any major city.

In 1307, the surprise choice to become Supreme Pontiff was the Archbishop of Bordeaux. On his promotion, Bertrand de Goth adopted the name of Clément V, before going on to introduce Christianity to China, and to make a non-ecclesiastical mark on the world with two very different wines. In Pessac, he is commemorated by Château Pape-Clément, where he first planted vines in 1300. Across at the southern end of the Rhône Valley, he is the Pope who briefly ran an exiled papacy in Avignon and established

vineyards in the nearby pebbly land that now bears the name of Châteauneuf du Pape. Pape-Clément, which today can be seen behind its railings on a busy suburban road, close to the younger estate of Haut-Brion, has a quaintly "olde-worlde" turreted tower topped by a pepperpot roof and weathervane dating from the late 19th century.

The fact that vines were grown in Pessac, on what are now the western outskirts of Bordeaux, long before they were in many other parts of the Graves and most of the Médoc, is explained by the presence both of a gravelly *croupe* – a slightly higher and thus healthier piece of land – and of a spring that was famous in the days of the Roman occupation. In fact, before taking on the name of its papal owner, the estate was known as Ste Marie de Bel Air.

Even if this was not the *vin clémentin* referred to by the writer Rabelais in the early 16th century, the prestige that Clément brought to the surrounding region seems to have encouraged others to grow grapes and to make wine. Among the *Anciens Réglements de la Ville de Bordeaux* – "Old Rules of the City of Bordeaux" – depicted on a medieval print was one that forbade innkeepers to blend "wines from the Médoc and other regions with those of the Graves". There was also a ban on the promotion of "wines from other places and growths as Graves wines".

would have been "Graves Claret". There was one notable exception to this rule, however, as Samuel Pepys discovered on a visit to the latter establishment on April 11th 1663, when he enjoyed "a sort of French wine, called Ho Bryan, that hath as good and most particular taste that I ever met with".

Over the following two centuries, these wines became the best known in Bordeaux and commanded the highest prices. As elsewhere, however, the only estates that had a reputation of their own were ones such as Pape-Clément and Ste-Croix whose wines were exclusively for the lips of the clergy and their guests. Everything else was simply sold under the name of the region where it was made. So, the wine that 16th- and 17th-century customers of London taverns such as *The Mouth* and *The Royall Oak* would have called for by the jug

Pepys, who, incidentally, had vowed just three weeks earlier to give up wine completely, was not the only person to get the name of Haut-Brion wrong in the days before wines were sold with printed labels. Other misspellings, including Aubryan, Oberon and O'Brien, merely indicate how successful the estate's owner Arnaud de Pontac and his son François-Auguste were in their efforts to establish what was effectively the world's first branded wine. Haut-Brion is named after the *brion* – the "little rise of ground ... scarce fit to bear anything" – close to the village of Pessac, and

57

Veraison – the moment in August when ripening grapes (opposite) develop their colour – is always a highlight of the vinegrower's year. These Semillon grapes (above) at Château du Seuil will produce rich, peachy wine.

described in 1677 by John Locke. The English philosopher also observantly took note of the "white sand, mixed with gravel".

The ground that so impressed Locke has not changed, and the château itself still looks from a distance as though it is wallowing in a sea of vines, but in other ways the view today is very different. Where there would have been trees and vineyards, there are now undistinguished houses and office blocks. For a somewhat more interesting taste of Pessac suburbia, it is worth visiting the *Quartier Moderne Frugès*, a collection of 51 pastel-coloured homes designed in the 1920s by Le Corbusier.

La Mission Haut-Brion may once have been part of the same estate as Château Haut-Brion, its neighbour and long-time rival on the other side of the stream of Citroëns and Renaults that roar along the Avenue Jean Jaurès. Alternatively (opinions vary), it may have enjoyed a separate existence until coming under the same ownership in 1983. In any case, it is a very different-looking building, constructed, along with a chapel, by its ecclesiastical owners, *les Precheurs de la Mission*, at the beginning of the 18th century. And it produces a discernibly different, more obviously opulent and more perfumed wine.

Defining the style of the wines produced in the Graves is actually quite tricky. The reds seem to mix the blackcurrant-and-cigar-box character of the Médoc with the richness of Pomerol and the earthiness of St Émilion, so spotting them "blind" is often a challenge. Even before the trend toward making ultra-concentrated wines, the natural weight of good Graves seemed to vary. Haut-Brion's "particular taste" and the deep colour referred to by other early fans probably owed much to the fact that de Pontac simply took more care over the way that it was made, but the estate's wines still have a massive, initially stand-offish character and flavours of black cherry and strawberry that set them apart in blind tastings from the other first growths and from Haut-Brion's neighbours. Domaine de Chevalier's red, by contrast, is subtler in style, with more raspberry notes; I always think of it as a Burgundy-drinker's Bordeaux.

French traditionalists would hate to see the wines of Bordeaux and Burgundy being compared to each other; when I told a prominent Burgundian that I believed

58

BOTH THE PHILOSOPHER JOHN LOCKE AND THOMAS JEFFERSON WERE STRUCK BY THE DISTINCTIVE GRAVELLY SOIL OF THE VINEYARDS AT CHÂTEAU HAUT-BRION WHEN THEY MADE THEIR RESPECTIVE VISITS IN THE 17TH AND 18TH CENTURIES.

Haut-Brion Blanc to be a match for any Corton-Charlemagne or Montrachet, he looked at me as if I had suggested that Dickens was a rival to Zola. But, at their best, the whites of the Graves are unquestionably among the greatest wines in the world. The precise flavour will partly depend on how great a role is played by the fresh, leafy Sauvignon Blanc (the proportion can vary from 25 per cent to 100 per cent) and the richer, peachier, more waxy Semillon, and on how much use has been made of new oak. The keynote should be a complex combination of peach, greengage and apple, with the richness of cream and – after a few years – the roundness of honey.

The semi-sweet Graves Supérieur produced in the southern part of the region should have honey too; unfortunately, good examples of this *appellation* are as rare as the style is unfashionable. This is an instance where the word *supérieur* could all too often be replaced with *inférieur*. There are some delicious dry red and white wines being made in the southern Graves nowadays, but none can compete with the best efforts of the north of the region. This explains why, in 1987, a set of communes in the north created a wholly separate *appellation*, naming it after both Pessac and the more southerly country town of Léognan. This division of the Graves only served to confirm what the region's vinous authorities had already decided in 1959, when 16 Pessac-Léognan châteaux were officially recognized as Crus Classés. This classification, however, leaves plenty to be desired – especially given the advances in white-wine making over the last half-century. What justification is there today for declaring both the red and white wines from Domaine de Chevalier to be *classé*, while the sublime whites from Haut-Brion and the reliably excellent Smith-Haut-Lafitte, La Louvière and Fieuzal remain as unclassified as the most basic whites in the region? A reclassification – which would include a few exceptional châteaux in the southern Graves, such as Chantegrive, Seuil, Clos Floridène and Rahoul, as well as previous omissions in Pessac-Léognan – has been described as being "imminent" for almost as long as I can remember. No one is holding their breath.

In the meantime, as elsewhere in Bordeaux, I'm happy to ignore the official rankings and to explore the region and its wines for myself. Of Haut-Brion and Pape-Clément's other neighbours in Pessac, La

61

Tour-Haut-Brion, Laville-Haut-Brion and Les Carmes Haut-Brion, which is said to owe a warmer microclimate to the houses by which it is surrounded, are the only classic vineyards to have withstood the urban sprawl. To find the other great châteaux of Pessac-Léognan, you have to head further south, out of the suburbs and into the sudden greenness of the communes of Léognan, Villenave-d'Ornon, Cadaujac and Martillac.

The landscape is unlike most of the rest of Bordeaux. There are gentle hills and vales and clumps of trees that frequently hide one château from another. Château Carbonnieux, one of the oldest, largest and – in recent years – finest estates in the region, has an attractively unostentatious building and courtyard, and vineyards that date from the 12th century and straddle the border between Léognan and Villenave-d'Ornon. In the 18th century, the estate belonged to Benedictine monks who used to sell their white wine to customers including a French-born woman in Constantinople who cannily referred to the wine as "*eau minérale de*

LIKE MOST OF ITS NEIGHBOURS IN THE GRAVES, THE DOMAINE DE CHEVALIER NEEDS TWO BARREL HALLS: ONE EACH FOR ITS RED AND WHITE WINE. THE RED WINE PRODUCED HERE IS ONE OF THE MOST SUBTLE IN THE REGION.

Despite their romantic image, most of the wine châteaux of Bordeaux are disappointingly mundane. The turreted and moated Château Olivier (above) is a glorious exception. At the end of a long day, the harvesters return to Château Olivier (opposite). Many other estates now use machines to pick their grapes.

Carbonnieux en Guienne" when serving it to appreciative guests such as the Ottoman emperor.

Curiously, for a long time the vinous potential of other parts of this region remained unrecognized. To the west of Carbonnieux, surrounded by a narrow moat and looking just like a toy castle, stands Château Olivier. Built in the Middle Ages and now classified as a national monument, Olivier only began to make wine seriously in the 19th century. Prior to that, grapes were secondary to other forms of farming. Château Haut-Bailly — a regional rarity in producing exclusively (great) red wine — was established only in the mid-1800s and its slightly stern, red-roofed building dates from the end of that century. Its land was once part of the same estate as that which is now called Château Larrivet-Haut-Brion (but which, prior to a legal tussle with Château Haut-Brion, used to bear the name Haut-Brion-Larrivet). Of such confusions is Bordeaux made.

Further south, on the other side of Léognan, and in the heart of pine woods that were originally cleared in the 18th century, stands Domaine de Chevalier. Far less massive than the wines of Haut-Brion or Pape-Clément, the reds and particularly the whites here have the distinction of living longer, developing more dramatically and shining more brightly in poor vintages than most of their peers. Asking even highly skilled tasters to guess the age of an old Domaine de Chevalier is one of the oldest in the Bordeaux bag of tricks.

65

66   Nearby, Smith-Haut-Lafitte sits on its own little *fitte* — hillock — and, following enthusiastic restoration, boasts a handsome white manor house and an eminently visitable part-timbered betowered building that now looks for all the world like something Hollywood would create for a medieval epic. It is actually far younger than it looks, but vines were grown here in the 12th century and the estate had already established its own identity in 1549, 171 years before it was bought by a Scotsman called George Smith. Today, the château's dynamic owners have resurrected and updated a tradition begun at Pape-Clément more than 1,700 years ago. Instead of offering healthy spring water, Smith-Haut-Lafitte now proposes wine made from organically-grown grapes and a spa specializing in the beneficial properties of oil extracted from their pips. The white is gently exotic, with a subtle pineappley note, while the red can have a delicious raspberry-mulberry character.

After the Disney-like appeal of Smith-Haut-Lafitte, La Louvière — whose name refers to the wolves that were

BEYOND THE SHADOW OF WELSH SCULPTOR BARRY FLANAGAN'S LEAPING HARE (ABOVE), STAND THE "OLDE-WORLDE" BUILDINGS OF CHÂTEAU SMITH-HAUT-LAFITTE, ONE OF THE MOST VISITED ESTATES IN THE REGION. THE IMPECCABLY MAINTAINED VINEYARDS HERE (OPPOSITE) ARE AMONG THE FIRST IN BORDEAUX TO BE FARMED ORGANICALLY.

hunted in the woods by which it is still partly
surrounded – offers a return to classicism with the same
kind of handsome looks as Château Margaux and the
Grand Théâtre in Bordeaux. This last resemblance is
hardly coincidental because it was designed – in 1798 –
by Victor Louis, the architect of that building, or by one
of his pupils. André Lurton, who, with his sons Jacques
and François, is responsible for restoring the building
and for transforming La Louvière's wines into ones that
should be given instant reclassification, also deserves
credit for defeating a powerful coalition of interests that
wanted to replace the vineyards of Martillac with a
science park and a housing estate. The example that the
Lurtons set as winemakers here, and in Entre-Deux-
Mers at Château Bonnet, cannot be exaggerated. Their
success with La Louvière, Couhins-Lurton, Cruzeau
and Rochemorin in the 1970s and 1980s helped to lay
the dull, grubbily over-sulphured whites of the past into
the mausoleum where they belonged. The pioneering
property alongside which La Louvière often seems to
march is Château Fieuzal, an estate whose modernity is
proclaimed by a stylish modern château with a pillared

69

entrance that casts its reflection prettily on an ornamental pond. Both the reds and whites are among the most reliable in the region.

Further south, beginning close to the town of Podensac (where Le Corbusier left his mark in the form of a water tower), the region of Cérons deserves more attention than it usually gets. This is old winegrowing country that already had a reputation – as Sirione – in the third century. The 12th-century Romanesque churches in Cérons itself and nearby Illats and the remains of windmills provide ample evidence of the prosperity the region once enjoyed. There are gravelly *croupes* here and limestone soil that can potentially produce luscious wines to rival those of Barsac, a little further south. Unfortunately, the steady decline in popularity of sweet wines and the possibility – legally denied to the châteaux of Sauternes and Barsac – of producing easy-

to-sell dry red and white Graves from these vineyards has helped turn the Cérons *appellation* into a rarity. For a taste of what the region can do in the right hands, buy a wine from the Château de Cérons, opposite the village church, or from the Château du Seuil, and leave it for a while; good vintages age brilliantly.

One of the best-known châteaux in the Graves – and certainly the most frequently visited – produces no great wine. The Château de Labrède, however, does have two other attributes: it was the home of the philosopher-lawyer-statesman Montesquieu and is a remarkably beautiful building – one of the few that really does look like the kind of castle from which a distressed damsel might be fruitfully rescued. Surrounded by a moat and parkland and approached via a small bridge, it has a set of pointed towers and a courtyard where, some three quarters of a century

BORDEAUX IS NOT ALL VINES. CORN (ABOVE) GROWS WELL NEAR THE LITTLE-KNOWN REGION OF CÉRONS. FRANCE'S HIGH-SPEED TRAIN, THE TGV (OPPOSITE), HURTLES PAST THE VINEYARDS OF THE CHÂTEAU DU SEUIL IN CÉRONS.

before the Revolution, one can easily imagine the great man descending from his library to entertain guests with elegant pronouncements about freedom. Or perhaps rehearsing his own description of Labrède: "definitely Gothic, but set off by a charming park which I laid out to a plan I discovered in England ... . Nature ... appears as if rising unadorned from her bed, clothed only in a dressing gown". In Montesquieu's day, much of the wine he would have served, drunk and sold came from vineyards four kilometres further north in Martillac where he had an estate known as La Tour after its 12th-century tower. Today, the fruit of those vines goes to make recommendable, usually middleweight, reds and whites under the name of Château La Tour-Martillac. Almost as venerable as that tower, the Château de Roquetaillade, though much restored by

Viollet-le-Duc in the 19th century, was originally built in 1307 and still offers visitors a chance to imagine life in the days when vinegrowing was merely one of the various forms of agriculture in this part of Bordeaux.

Before leaving the Graves to head further inland, I have to recommend a brief diversion to Bazas, to which I was directed by the British writer Pamela Vandyke Price. You could search most guide books in vain for even a mention of this town, but it was once significant enough as a rural centre to give its name to the entire Bazadais region that is still referred to on maps. It was also sufficiently important to justify a fine and surprisingly sizeable cathedral, parts of which date back to the 13th century. Bazas's arcades and narrow streets are full of unexpected delights — just like the rest of the Graves.

73

TWO OF THE FINEST BUILDINGS IN BORDEAUX: THE 14TH-CENTURY CHÂTEAU DE ROQUETAILLADE (OPPOSITE) PRODUCES GOOD WINE, WHILE THE MUCH-VISITED CHÂTEAU LABRÈDE (ABOVE) IS BETTER KNOWN AS THE HOME OF MONTESQUIEU.

CHAPTER FOUR

SAUTERNES AND BARSAC

Of all the vaunted luxuries in the world, the luscious liquid gold of fine Sauternes is one of the most extraordinary. Its production relies heavily on the unpredictable development of an ugly mould on the surface of the grapes — and on the patience and care of producers who turn those grapes into wine. Curiously, the source of this not-quite-annual alchemy is one of the most modest and peaceful corners of Bordeaux: a region that offers a surprising contrast to the landscapes of the Médoc and St Émilion.

A PLAQUE AT CHÂTEAU CLIMENS (ABOVE), THE BARSAC ESTATE THAT MAKES SOME OF THE FINEST OF ALL SAUTERNES. THE WINE AT CHÂTEAU DE MALLE (OPPOSITE) IS NOT QUITE AS FINE BUT THE BUILDINGS ARE MORE SPECTACULAR.

If I wanted to hide away for a few days, Sauternes and its neighbour Barsac might be the perfect place to do so. This is one of the most bucolic parts of Bordeaux: a small area of tiny hamlets consisting of a few houses to the side of narrow, winding roads that appear to lead nowhere, and along which one wouldn't be surprised to find smock-wearing goatherds leading their flocks. The vineyards, behind their low stone walls, have a cosy, timeless feeling too, which sets them in a totally different era from the *autoroute* that bisects the region on its way from Bordeaux to Toulouse (see map, p.55).

It is very difficult nowadays to enter this magic little corner by accident; there are far too many signs advertising the two *appellations* and their châteaux. Historically, though, the five villages that now come under the Sauternes *appellation* were simply a higher-quality part of the southern Graves. Preignac, close to the river, had vineyards as early as the eighth century and local wine would have been shipped from the little port of Barsac, where a grassy bank is now more likely to welcome visiting picnickers. We have no way of knowing quite how the wine that was produced in those early days might have

AUTUMN MIST OVER THE RIVER CIRON (OPPOSITE) HELPS TO CREATE THE "NOBLE ROT" WHICH IS REQUIRED TO MAKE GREAT SAUTERNES. THE QUIET PORT DE BARSAC (ABOVE), WHERE BOATS WOULD HAVE LOADED BARRELS OF THE REGION'S WINE.

tasted or looked, but, by the 18th century, there is little doubt that Sauternes was white and quite sweet, though not lusciously so. Like whites from the rest of the Graves region, it would have been produced from grapes that had been left to become very ripe before they were picked. The hills in Sauternes and Barsac would simply have ripened the fruit a little more fully than elsewhere, helping to make for wine like the 1784, which Thomas Jefferson bought and unevocatively described as "excellent" and "very fine".

For the wines to have the intensity of flavour and sweetness and the complex mixture of honey, dried apricots and peaches we would expect today, the grapes need to be affected by a benign fungus called *Botrytis cinerea*, to produce *pourriture noble* – "noble rot". This dark-khaki furry mould (see photo, above), which only appears naturally in a small number of regions, makes the fruit look so unprepossessing that only courage or desperation would drive anyone to imagine using them to make wine. Even in our own era, Robert Mondavi recalls having to harvest and crush nobly-rotten grapes from the Napa Valley secretly – to avoid the attention of

Food and Drug Administration officials, who, he felt sure, would have put a halt to such a self-evidently unhealthy activity. The first people who, like the cheesemakers of Roquefort and Stilton, learned that a little of the right kind of mould could be a good thing were probably the 17th-century winemakers of Tokaji in Hungary. At Schloss Johannisberg in Germany, the cellar-master accidentally made the same discovery in 1775 when instructions to begin harvesting were delayed and he had no choice but to treat the ugly-looking little berries as though they were fresh, healthy ones.

Curiously, a similar story is told at Château d'Yquem. Apparently, in 1847, the Marquis Bertrand de Lur-Saluces, head of the family that had owned the estate since the 16th century, spent longer than he should on an autumn sales trip to Russia. By the time he returned, the fungus had appeared on a large proportion of the grapes that were waiting to be picked – and performed its alchemy on them. A dozen years later, the wine made from those mouldy grapes would be sold to the Czar's brother for the then-unheard-of sum of 20,000 gold francs per *tonneau*, or 16 francs per bottle

78

– four times the price of previous vintages. It is tempting to think that this was also the wine that was tasted by the brokers of Bordeaux when they came to draw up the 1855 Classification for the *Exposition Universelle* in Paris. It might explain how they came to name Yquem as Bordeaux's only Grand Premier Cru Classé – thus ranking it a notch above Latour, Lafite, Margaux and Haut-Brion.

Less romantically, it is quite possible that a well-travelled Dutch merchant with a sweet tooth might have told the Sauternais what he had seen in Hungary or on the Rhine, and I find it hard to believe that, when a man called Focke bought the nearby Château La Tour Blanche in the 1830s, he did not introduce the concept of using nobly-rotten grapes from his native Germany. One interesting explanation, raised by Hugh Johnson, for this historical vagueness is that cellarmasters saw something shameful in the use of the mouldy grapes and so kept the practice secret. How, though, would it have gone unnoticed for long within a small community?

However and whenever the Sauternais began to exploit the noble rot that is fostered by the mists that rise in the autumn from the nearby River Ciron and which is perfectly suited to the Semillon and Sauvignon Blanc grapes that are grown here, it is clear that the leading estates had all mastered the making of fine,

intense sweet wine in time to take their place beneath Yquem in the 1855 Classification. Today, while the top châteaux of the Médoc, St Émilion and Pomerol compete on more or less level terms, Yquem's wine still stands above its neighbours', in much the same way that the turreted 16th-century château on its – by Bordeaux standards, near-mountainous 75-metre – hill overlooks the rest of the *appellation*. If the combination of the particular aspect and steepness of the slopes that surround Yquem and its clay and sandy gravel soil is largely responsible for the quality of the wines here, credit also has to go to the owners for their efforts. Chauvinist claims for the natural aptitude of Bordeaux's land – *terroir* – for winegrowing need to be balanced against the fact that Château d'Yquem benefits from, and has to maintain, no less than 100 kilometres of drainage tiles which were installed in the 19th century.

Yields are pitifully low; each vine produces a scant eighth as much as its counterpart in the Médoc – less than a glass per vine – and the harvesting is ludicrously slow and labour-intensive, taking as long as two months, and as many as 12 or 13 *tries* – separate mini-harvests – to ensure that each bunch is at precisely the optimum level of ripeness and rot. Even more unusually, when the vintage as a whole fails to meet the required standard, Yquem simply doesn't release a wine at all. When

79

you take all of these factors into account and consider that good Sauternes will outlast any red Bordeaux and probably gain more from keeping, the apparently astronomical prices paid for bottles of Yquem at auction take on an entirely fresh perspective.

Standards at Yquem's neighbours are, however, very nearly as high, and prices are substantially lower. In fact, I'd go as far as to say that a bottle of wine from a vintage in the late 1990s from Coutet, Climens, Guiraud, Lafaurie-Peyraguey, Rayne-Vigneau, Rieussec, Suduiraut or La Tour Blanche is actually one of the bargains of the wine world. Choosing a favourite among these is often more a matter of individual taste or of one or other château's performance in a particular vintage, but Château de Malle and the medieval Château Lafaurie-Peyraguey compete for the prize of being the most beautiful. There are plenty of other smaller estates that produce good Sauternes but, like St Émilion, the *appellation* is a minefield replete with poor examples. As a rule, if you steer a path around the generic Sauternes in supermarkets you won't be denying yourself much pleasure; taking the opportunity to sample the wines on offer in the Maison de Sauternes in the village of Sauternes itself is, however, one of the most useful wine lessons you could take.

The little region of Barsac enjoys a form of open marriage with the rest of Sauternes. It was settled by the Romans and its wines were known in London significantly before the *vin de sauterne*. Today, it has a large church, a few shops and advertising hoardings, some of which look disconcertingly as though they were painted half a century ago. There is little encouragement to pause here. When compared to their neighbours, Barsac's vineyards seem to be plain and flat too — rather like those of Pomerol. But the subtle *croupe* and limestone soil contribute to a vibrant note that sets the wines of châteaux Coutet and Climens, in particular, apart from their peers. Producers here have the choice of labelling their wines as Barsac or Sauternes. When they or any other château in Sauternes choose to make a dry white wine, insane *appellation d'origine contrôlée* legislation obliges them to sell it as Bordeaux Blanc — just like the cheapest, most ordinary wine in the region. But a humble label is hardly likely to deter fans from buying fascinatingly individual wines such as Château d'Yquem's Ygrec and Rieussec's "R".

ONE OF THE SEVERAL MINI-HARVESTS — *TRIES* — THAT WILL GO INTO THE VINTAGE AT CHÂTEAU D'YQUEM. PICKING IN THIS WAY ENSURES THAT THE GRAPES ARE RIPE AND SUFFICIENTLY AFFECTED BY NOBLE ROT TO GIVE THE WINE ITS CHARACTER.

CHAPTER FIVE

ENTRE-DEUX-MERS

Often overlooked by visiting wine lovers who are bedazzled by the wines and châteaux of
the more illustrious regions of Bordeaux, the historic area of Entre-Deux-Mers remains
something of a secret to be shared among people who know and live in Bordeaux. The
finest vineyards and producers in this tract of land between the Dordogne and Garonne
rivers today produce some of Bordeaux's best value reds and whites, and the countryside,
towns, churches and châteaux are among the most beautiful in the region.

CHÂTEAU DU MONT IN THE PREMIÈRES CÔTES DE BORDEAUX (ABOVE) IS ONE OF THIS AREA'S GROWING NUMBER OF
INCREASINGLY AMBITIOUS ESTATES. THE AUTUMNAL MORNING MIST, TO THE NORTH OF TARGON (OPPOSITE).

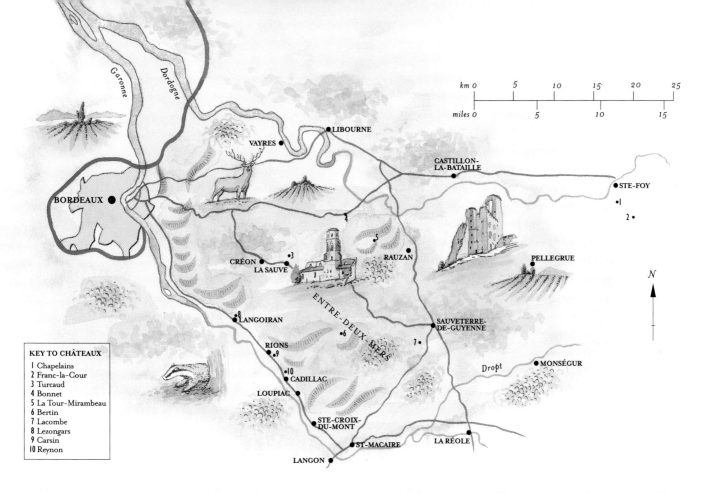

KEY TO CHÂTEAUX

1 Chapelains
2 Franc-la-Cour
3 Turcaud
4 Bonnet
5 La Tour-Mirambeau
6 Bertin
7 Lacombe
8 Lezongars
9 Carsin
10 Reynon

If any part of Bordeaux can be said to possess an appeal that significantly transcends its vineyards, it has to be the Entre-Deux-Mers, the region "between two seas" or, to be more precise, between the Garonne and Dordogne rivers. This is an area of tiny roads that wind through lush forests and between and over hills. There are some fairly large areas of vines here, but many of the vineyards are happened upon by chance – as are some of the prettiest villages, towns, châteaux, castles, abbeys and churches in Bordeaux.

The word "between" implies something transitory and the Entre-Deux-Mers is indeed an area that people have always tended to cross on their way from one place to another. Today, the journey usually involves a swift *autoroute* drive from Bordeaux inland to Libourne, St Émilion or Bergerac. Nine centuries ago, the people

THE MOULIN DE LOUBENS AND THE STREAM THAT CONTRIBUTES TO AN IDEAL MICROCLIMATE FOR SWEET WHITE WINE.

travelling through the region would have been footsore pilgrims on their way from Fraise and St Émilion to Santiago de Compostela in Spain. So many people undertook this pilgrimage that, between 1135 and 1140, a *Guide* – a precocious predecessor of the modern travel book – was actually produced and listed routes and places to stay. In the region of Bordeaux, the *Guide* helpfully pointed out, "the wine is excellent and fish plentiful, but the language is rough ...". One place where it would presumably have been less so was the Abbey of La Sauve Majeure, which was built in 1079 and offered sufficient space for a congregation of 2,000 made up of local inhabitants and pilgrims who received wooden bread boxes blessed by the priest. The abbey is in a poor state today, but the top of the tower dating from two centuries later is a fine place from which to survey the surrounding landscape and to imagine the armies of England and France who fought for possession of the region in the Hundred Years' War. The Entre-Deux-

Mers is scattered with fortified reminders of those battles, such as the ruined châteaux de Langoiran and Rauzan and the medieval walled town of Rions.

In more peaceful times the Entre-Deux-Mers benefited from the keenness of Bordeaux aristocrats to establish estates where they could get away from the city during the warm summer months. In a sense, the area took on a very similar role for them to the one played by Long Island for some of the richer inhabitants of Manhattan. And just as the modern money men of Wall Street might commission an architect to create a smart holiday home in the Hamptons, the lawyers and parliamentarians of Bordeaux built themselves some very attractive *chartreuses* – the local low, wide single- and two-storey country houses. There were vineyards too, but few of these were blessed with the soil or aspect required to make really good wine or to develop a reputation for themselves.

86

ONE OF THE MANY CARVED STONE CAPITALS IN THE RUINS OF LA SAUVE MAJEURE (ABOVE); 1,000 YEARS AGO THE ABBEY, (OPPOSITE) WELCOMED THOUSANDS OF WEARY PILGRIMS WHO PAUSED HERE ON THEIR WAY TO SANTIAGO DE COMPOSTELA.

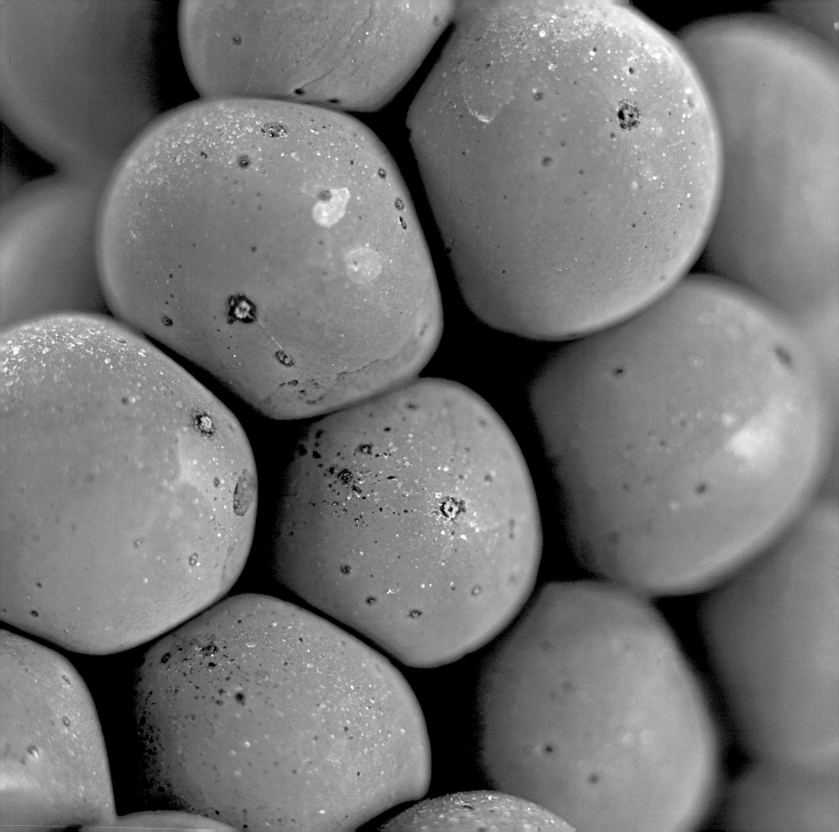

Today, much the same can be said for most of the land that falls under the Entre-Deux-Mers *appellation*; it's a place to produce medium-quality, undemanding red and white – in years when the sun shines sufficiently for the grapes to ripen. To achieve more than that, and to hit the bull's eye in trickier vintages, calls for unusually well-sited vines and unusually skilled winemakers. One place where these come together and are happily combined with a spectacular château is at Château Bonnet, home to the family of André Lurton, one of the heroes of Pessac-Léognan. Other similarly successful Entre-Deux-Mers producers include Camarsac, La Tour-Mirambeau and Turcaud.

Thanks to one of the many quirky little rules of *appellation* lore, red and rosé produced within the Entre-Deux-Mers *appellation* can be sold only as Bordeaux and is thus indistinguishable by its label from wine made anywhere else in the entire region. This is resented less than one might expect, as is indicated by the fact that many producers who might legally call their white "Entre-Deux-Mers" prefer, in any case, simply to offer it as white Bordeaux, reasoning that the more specific

CABERNET SAUVIGNON GRAPES AT CHÂTEAU ROUSTAING NEAR TARGON (OPPOSITE). CHÂTEAU BONNET (ABOVE), ONE OF THE MOST BEAUTIFUL ESTATES IN BORDEAUX — AND SOURCE OF SOME OF THE MOST RELIABLE AND FAIRLY PRICED WINE.

appellation adds no cachet to the liquid in the bottle. Even good wines, such as Dourthe's No 1 Bordeaux Blanc, that owe their flavour exclusively to Entre-Deux-Mers grapes, choose not to advertise their origins.

The *appellation* "Entre-Deux-Mers" may not always be taken seriously, but it is at least widely available. In contrast, there are several obscure *appellations* here whose existence is barely acknowledged. Ask a specialist wine merchant for an Entre-Deux-Mers-Haut-Benauge, a Bordeaux-Haut-Benauge, a Ste-Foy-Bordeaux, a Côtes de Bordeaux-St-Macaire or a Graves-de-Vayres and you are more likely to get a blank look than a bottle of wine. Vayres, in particular, is far better known for the magnificence of its royal château (now a conference centre), whose ornate gardens are set against the backdrop of the river. There are some good producers in these areas – châteaux Lacombe and Bertin are examples in Haut-Benauge – and a growing ambition to rise above the level of more basic Bordeaux. Ste Foy has created a quality charter for its wines that helps to make

APPELLATIONS HERE ARE OFTEN SEPARATED BY NOTHING MORE THAN A ROAD OR A LINE OF TREES. THE VINES IN THE FOREGROUND PRODUCE PREMIÈRES CÔTES DE BORDEAUX; THOSE IN THE DISTANCE MAKE ENTRE-DEUX-MERS.

them a more reliable buy than many a St Émilion Grand Cru. Châteaux Franc-la-Cour and Chapelains are worth looking out for here.

If these *appellations* are struggling to make their names, there is, however, a quartet of areas along the southern edge of the Entre-Deux-Mers region that already enjoys a following. Drive along the Garonne and you will understand why the wines of the Premières Côtes de Bordeaux, Cadillac, Loupiac and Ste Croix du Mont stand above most of their neighbours produced in vineyards further from the river. Even to the amateur, this feels like better vinegrowing country, with neat,

south-facing slopes on which grapes ripen more easily than on some of the flatter land of Entre-Deux-Mers.

The Premières Côtes de Bordeaux is the fastest rising star, thanks to the efforts of châteaux such as Reynon and Carsin, both of which produce rich reds and genuinely characterful whites that easily match wines from the supposedly smarter Graves vineyards across the river. The British-owned Château Lezongars, near the town of Langoiran, is also setting an example by producing minuscule quantities of intense red wine which is sold at high prices by Jean-Luc Thunevin, the man who made his name selling similarly tiny

93

LEFT TO RIGHT: TALL SEMILLON VINES GROWING AT CHÂTEAU DU MONT; A VIEW ACROSS THE GARONNE TO CADILLAC FROM CHÂTEAU DU SEUIL; THE ANNUAL CADILLAC CAR RALLY OUTSIDE CADILLAC (2003 IS THE CENTENARY OF THE MANUFACTURER); CLOSING A VAT AT CHÂTEAU CARSIN, ONE OF THE MOST MODERN WINERIES IN BORDEAUX.

amounts of an intense St Émilion called Château Valandraud (see p.110).

The advantage enjoyed by the Premières Côtes *appellation* over its more southerly neighbours is simple: nowadays there is a greater demand for red wine than for sweet white. If Sauternes producers sometimes struggle to survive, it is easy to imagine the plight of châteaux in Cadillac, Loupiac and Ste Croix du Mont, whose wines in recent years have been considered to be a poor man's alternative. But there's a lot of pride here, and a lot of history. Compared to the relatively humble communes of Sauternes or Barsac, Cadillac is a serious old fortified town, boasting an elegant 17th-century château with beautiful painted ceilings, as well as a spacious market square in which, 700 years ago, barrels of local wine would have been busily traded. Since

94

its recognition in 1973 as an *appellation*, Cadillac has mostly produced sweet but less than luscious white wine. There has been a recent renaissance here, however, led by estates such as Château du Juge, and Château Fayau, whose Sauternes-quality wine cheekily boasts a very Yquem-like label. Close by, Loupiac is home to some fine vineyards and producers — Loupiac-Gaudet, du Cros, Domaine du Noble and Clos Jean are all stars — and a mosaic-tiled Roman bath that reveals just how long ago its setting in the hills was first appreciated. In Ste Croix du Mont, the best wine is usually from the 17th-century Château Loubens, but Crabitan-Bellevue, Lousteau-Vieil and La Rame would all justify travelling to — rather than through — the region.

CHÂTEAU STE-CROIX-DU-MONT (ABOVE), SOURCE OF SOME OF BORDEAUX'S BETTER VALUE LATE-HARVEST SWEET WHITE WINE. A VINEYARD TO THE SOUTH OF CASTELVIEL (OPPOSITE) WHERE VINES ARE READY TO BE TRIMMED FOR SPRING.

CHAPTER SIX

LIBOURNE, ST ÉMILION AND POMEROL

96

For most of the last millennium, the Dordogne was a frontier between the two halves of

what we now know as Bordeaux. To the east of the river, on the so-called "Right Bank",

St Émilion and Pomerol grew up quite separately from their siblings, the Médoc and

Graves, and remained in their shadow. It was not until the latter years of the 20th century

that their highly distinctive wines finally began to attract the attention they deserved.

THE NEAT BLOCKS OF VINES IN ST ÉMILION (ABOVE). MOST ESTATES HERE PRODUCE LESS WINE THAN THEIR COUNTERPARTS
IN THE MÉDOC. THE ST ÉMILION SKYLINE (OPPOSITE) REVEALS THE TOWN'S MILITARY AND RELIGIOUS HISTORY.

For centuries, Libourne commanded traffic along the River Dordogne. Today it flourishes as a market town.

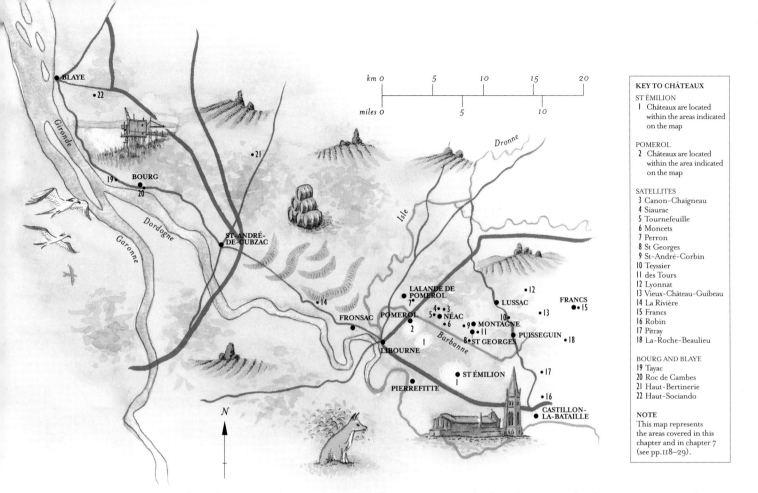

KEY TO CHÂTEAUX

ST ÉMILION
1   Châteaux are located
    within the areas indicated
    on the map

POMEROL
2   Châteaux are located
    within the area indicated
    on the map

SATELLITES
3   Canon-Chaigneau
4   Siaurac
5   Tournefeuille
6   Moncets
7   Perron
8   St Georges
9   St-André-Corbin
10 Teyssier
11 des Tours
12 Lyonnat
13 Vieux-Château-Guibeau
14 La Rivière
15 Francs
16 Robin
17 Pitray
18 La-Roche-Beaulieu

BOURG AND BLAYE
19 Tayac
20 Roc de Cambes
21 Haut-Bertinerie
22 Haut-Sociando

NOTE
This map represents
the areas covered in this
chapter and in chapter 7
(see pp.118–29).

Crossing the Dordogne and arriving in the Libournais is like straying into a different world. The landscapes – for there are several to be found here – are quite unlike most of the Médoc and Entre-Deux-Mers. There are – by the calm standards of the rest of Bordeaux – some dramatic slopes made up of soil that has more clay and sand and less obvious gravel than elsewhere in the region. The châteaux tend to be less imposing too: some of the most famous look disconcertingly like nothing so much as humble farmworkers'

cottages. And, of course, the least experienced wine drinker can often recognize that the Bordeaux produced here is far more influenced by the prevalent Merlot grape which is responsible for a style and flavour that isn't to be found on the other, more Cabernet-dominated, side of the Dordogne and Gironde. Softness and approachability are the keynotes, along – in more recent vintages – with surprising amounts of spice. If any of Bordeaux's wines can be described as sexy, this is where they are most likely to be found.

The original gateway to the vineyards of St Émilion and Pomerol would have been the ancient little river port of Pierrefitte. This role was soon supplanted, however, by Libourne, which was founded in the 13th century by an Englishman called Roger de Leybourne at the meeting point of the Dordogne and the narrower River Isle, which allowed access to regions further north. As Libourne developed as a citadel, it gradually gained as much of a monopoly over the trade in the wines of this region as Bordeaux held over the Médoc and Graves. Even today, my first stop when I want to sample the latest vintage from the top châteaux in St Émilion and Pomerol is the quayside tasting room of a merchant called Jean-Pierre Moueix.

Libourne has always been one of my favourite places in all of Bordeaux. An unspoiled country town bordered to one side by the quietly flowing, tree-fringed river, it has taken on neither the bourgeois airs and graces of Bordeaux itself nor the tourist-trap trappings of St Émilion. It remains what it has always been: home of a compact market where, thrice a week, local residents buy locally grown food from stalls that pack the central Place Abel Surchamp so tightly that some have had to be tucked beneath the arches of the 15th-century Hôtel de Ville. The town of St Émilion itself is actually about five kilometres away as the crow flies, but its vineyards and those of Pomerol begin almost as soon as the last houses of Libourne stop.

St Émilion is a big *appellation*. There are some 800 châteaux which collectively produce 30 million bottles of exclusively red wine, which find their way into almost every restaurant, supermarket, liquor store and specialist wine merchant on the planet. More wine is made here than in all four of the top communes of the Médoc combined, or all two dozen village *appellations* of Burgundy's Côte d'Or.

Despite its international renown, however, I perversely like to think of St Émilion as one of Bordeaux's secrets.

Visitors see the hilltop Roman town itself, with its maze of narrow cobbled alleys, steps and courtyards, its duochrome pattern of terracotta roofs and creamy walls, its extraordinary church, and the ruined wall and tower, which collectively serve as welcoming beacons. They remember the restaurants and cafés and the wine shops which are eager to ship their wares throughout the world, and they probably recall visiting one of the châteaux whose wines are stored in caves with smooth walls that were carved by the Romans two milliennia ago.

101

THE TASTING ROOM OF THE LIBOURNE MERCHANTS, J-P MOUEIX (OPPOSITE) IS AS MUCH OF A MECCA FOR WINE MERCHANTS AS THE MONUMENTS OF ST ÉMILION ARE FOR TOURISTS. THIS IS WHERE NEW VINTAGES OF WINES SUCH AS CHÂTEAU PÉTRUS ARE FIRST TASTED. NEARBY, THE STALLHOLDERS OF THE MARKET ON THE PLACE DES ARMES (ABOVE) DISPLAY THEIR WARES.

THE TILED ROOFS OF THE LITTLE TOWN OF ST ÉMILION
HAVE REMAINED UNCHANGED OVER THE CENTURIES.

And of course these are all genuine images of St Émilion, but they are like pieces of a mosaic; look a little further and you'll find a few more that are quite different. For example, just around the corner from the Couvent des Cordeliers's Roman cellar, there's a nondescript private house in whose converted garage is produced Château Valandraud, one of the most recently launched and most sought-after wines in the world. Go looking for some of St Émilion's other estates and you will more than likely become lost in a skein of country lanes. Some châteaux sit commandingly at the top of a hill; others punctuate a plain where there is scarcely the faintest suspicion of an incline. The more time you spend here and the more wines you taste, the more you realize that St Émilion and its wines are really rather hard to pin down, a mixture of often strongly contrasting personalities.

Where to start? Well, despite the tourist traps, there cannot be anywhere better than the town itself. This is, after all, close to where the Biturica vine was first planted and where Ausonius (see p.14) is said to have had one of his villas and, quite possibly, some of his vineyards. The reason for the uncertainty about the

103

Roman poet's links with St Émilion, as the Bordeaux authority Clive Coates points out, partly lies in the proud description he left of the reflection of his vines on the surface of the "yellowing Garonne". Even allowing for a little poetic licence, the nearest waterway is the Dordogne and even that is

well over two kilometres away. In fact, we know that, while his father, a doctor, had vines on the Garonne which Ausonius would have inherited, the poet also bought other pieces of land, one of which might easily have been at St Émilion. And even if this were not the case, the column, mosaic floor depicting grapes on a vine, *lagares* (stone troughs in which grapes would have been trodden by foot), and other Gallo-Roman ruins discovered in the grounds of Château La Gaffelière all prove that an important citizen certainly owned a sizeable villa just beneath the present-day vineyards of Château Ausone. Other archeological discoveries indicate that the Romans grew vines on the plateau behind Ausone, close to its neighbour Belair, planting them in straight trenches dug into the rock and lined by pieces of limestone carved from nearby caves which, in turn,

were used for storage. So popular did this cave-carving become over the years that some of the region's vineyards are now bizarrely suspended on stone pillars like hanging gardens.

Early Christians also carved out grottoes – to make places of prayer. Most famously, the eighth-century hermit, Aemilianus, who gave his name to St Émilion (previously called Lucianacum), lived in a shelter he had hewn out of limestone with his own hands. Émilion, as he is now known, was a pious monk who stopped here on a pilgrimage from his native Brittany to Santiago de Compostela and decided to stay; his touchingly simple cave and stone bed can still be visited at the Chapelle de la Trinité. Appropriately enough, the beautiful huge medieval church that stands in the heart of St Émilion today is an *église monolithe* dug into the side of a hill – and boasting an arch decorated by finely carved, if now often headless, saints.

Partly attracted by stories of a hermit who turned pieces of wood into loaves of bread for the poor and shared his own food with the birds, several monastic orders laid down their roots in the region, including

104

one whose abbey was almost completely destroyed in the Hundred Years' War. All that remains today is the impressive single wall — the three-arched "Grandes Murailles" — close to the roundabout at the northern entrance to the town. Like the ruins of Châteauneuf du Pape, it serves as one of the wine

world's more instantly memorable totems. St Émilion's other symbol is the severe square tower of the Château du Roy, on the edge of the town, which was built by the often forgotten English king Henry III.

This is the point from which, every year, a group of men in long red gowns modelled on ones worn 800 years ago ceremonially proclaim the beginning of the harvest. In 1199, King John gave St Émilion's wealthier citizens — known as the Jurade, because they had sworn (*juré*) allegiance — the right to administer their region. Among the Jurade's responsibilities was the testing of each vintage. Wines that were thought to be good

enough received a *marque du vinetier* certificate; those that weren't were destroyed. In 1948, the winegrowers of St Émilion resurrected and co-opted the Jurade for themselves as a largely promotional body that also takes responsibility for overseeing the quality of the wines coming from a region that, they proudly point out, has almost precisely the same borders as the one of eight centuries earlier. In fact, the area over which the original Jurade held sway would have had far fewer vineyards than the St Émilion of today. In an ideal world, the modern *appellation* would be smaller and would exclude the poorer, flatter, sandier-soil vineyards of the plain. This, in turn, would make it easier for the Jurade to disassociate the *appellation* from the annual flood of sub-standard, dull, earthy, St Émilion on sale in all those supermarkets and liquor stores.

Essentially, today, the region's vineyards are split geologically into three quite separate sections. At the top

105

St Émilion is named after a pious monk; this barrel (opposite) has its own religious associations, being produced and matured at Château Valandraud to strict kosher standards. Wearing their Medieval costumes, the Jurade of St Émilion (above) launch the harvest from the roof of the Château du Roy.

CHÂTEAU AUSONE, ONE OF THE SMALLEST ESTATES IN BORDEAUX, OWES ITS NAME TO THE ROMAN POET AUSONIUS.

— in terms of both altitude and quality — is the "Montagne", an area that covers the hill on which the town of St Émilion was built, the plateau that surrounds it, and the "Côtes" — the limestone slopes immediately to the south, south-west and south-east of the town. Further north, there is more clay and sand — and fewer top-class wines; while, frankly, much of the land to the west is simply too sandy to produce really fine Bordeaux. This description makes St Émilion sound a little like that other old wine region, the Côte d'Or in Burgundy, where the finest vineyards — the Grands and Premiers Crus — occupy the best strip along a slope that runs

more or less consistently southward from Dijon to Santenay. But St Émilion isn't nearly as straightforward as that. If you were to plot on a map the locations of the châteaux that are acknowledged to make the top wines in the *appellation*, you would find some of them to be surprisingly widely spread.

At the summit of the hill, to the south of St Émilion, close to the town and clustered together, there are châteaux Ausone, Belair, Canon and Magdelaine. By the end of the 20th century, the tiny (seven-hectare) estate of Ausone had regained its place at Bordeaux's top table, but during the 1980s and early 1990s its wines

UNLIKE THEIR FAR YOUNGER COUNTERPARTS IN THE MÉDOC AND GRAVES, SOME OF THE FINEST VINEYARDS IN ST ÉMILION
HAVE ORIGINS THAT ARE PROVED BY ARCHEOLOGICAL RUINS TO STRETCH BACK TO THE DAYS OF THE ROMAN EMPIRE.

failed to impress either those who like traditional elegant Bordeaux or fans of the richer, more modern style. Now, though, the 2,000 cases of wine it produces are the epitome of St Émilion at its best — an iron fist in a velvet glove, and a perfect *ménage à trois* of the damsony Merlot, the spicier, more blackcurranty Cabernet Franc and the limestone and clay slope on which they are planted.

Despite its ancient connections and modern reputation, Ausone's history as the source of truly great wine can only really be traced back to the middle of the 19th century. Belair, next door, is far older, and had a reputation for making the region's finest red in the mid-1700s. Today, in the château's labyrinthine caves, a bearded, monk-like giant called Pascal Delbeck presides over barrels of softly mineral, and curiously almost Burgundian, wine. I like Belair but have to admit that in an age of richer, fruitier, oakier flavours, its style is almost resolutely unfashionable. Château Magdelaine, which is made under the supervision of Jean-Claude Berrouet, who is better known for his efforts at Pétrus, falls somewhere between the style of its two neighbours, with a delicacy and perfumed spice that partly comes from the higher proportion of Merlot. The last in this hilltop quartet is Canon, which owes its name and its handsome building to Jacques Kanon, a privateer — or,

as some would say, pirate — who bought the estate in 1760, and is remembered for freeing his black slave before selling the château and sailing off to Haiti. The wines — back on form after a poor patch in the 1980s — are among the most complex and long-lived in the region.

Before moving down a little to the Côtes, I suppose we really ought to pause for a moment to look at the way in which St Émilion classifies its wines. To be quite honest, I've been putting off doing so, because it involves diving into some of the more murkily frustrating bits of Gallic wine legislation. None of the châteaux of St Émilion was named as a Grand Cru in 1855, most likely because the brokers of Bordeaux who drew up the Classification for the *Exposition Universelle* had little experience of dealing with them. Extraordinary though it may appear, as Clive Coates points out, the first bridge over the Garonne at Bordeaux wasn't built until the era of Napoleon; until the early 1800s the wines of St Émilion and Pomerol would have been the almost exclusive preserve of the brokers of Libourne. Whatever the reason, it was not until 1954 that a classification for St Émilion was drawn up. But starting late had an advantage: recommendably and uniquely in Bordeaux, it was decided to review this list every decade and this, after a bumpy start, is precisely what now happens.

108

AT CHÂTEAU BELAIR, ONE OF THE OLDEST ESTATES IN ST ÉMILION, WINE THAT HAS BEEN FERMENTED IN MODERN STAINLESS STEEL TANKS (LEFT), IS CAREFULLY AND PATIENTLY ALLOWED TO MATURE IN CELLARS (RIGHT) THAT WERE ORIGINALLY CARVED OUT OF THE LIMESTONE HILLS OVERLOOKING THE TOWN BY THE ROMANS MORE THAN TWO THOUSAND YEARS AGO.

So far, so clear. From here on it becomes a little more confusing. In its current incarnation, there are 13 Premiers Grands Crus Classés, which themselves fall into a pair of sections: two châteaux get the suffix "A" (Ausone and Cheval Blanc) and 11 (including Angélus, Belair, Canon, Figeac and Pavie) get the suffix "B". (Don't go looking for the suffixes on the labels, by the way; you won't find them.) Beneath these, there are 55

Grands Crus Classés (including Canon-la-Gaffelière, La Dominique and Troplong-Mondot). Wines from some 130 châteaux that fall outside this hierarchy are, however, allowed to call themselves "Grand Cru", provided the vintage in question has satisfied the less than demanding requirements of a blind tasting. Few true St Émilion enthusiasts would trust an unfamiliar Grand Cru enough to order it from a wine list; most would be ready to consider a Grand Cru Classé. To complicate matters even further, in the late 1980s an iconoclastic former bank clerk-turned-wine merchant called Jean-Luc Thunevin kicked another dent into the St Émilion classification system by buying up several patches of vines and using their grapes to produce an entirely new wine called Château Valandraud in the garage of his house in the middle of St Émilion. (There is no château, but the same can be said of Château Léoville-Barton.) Like Le Pin, the Pomerol on which it was partly modelled, this wine was made with meticulous care in tiny quantities (fewer than 750 cases) and in an immediately impressive, ultra-concentrated, oaky style that struck precisely the right note with a new generation of drinkers in the USA and Asia. Today, Valandraud and its successors, such as Le Dome, Quinault l'Enclos and La Mondotte, are among the priciest wines in Bordeaux, and none of them relies for its sales on any kind of classification at all.

The influence of these wines and of the popularity they command has been felt throughout Bordeaux, but arguably nowhere more so than in St Émilion where the owners of even some of the oldest estates now harvest later and make more use of new oak in order to offer wines with richer, more intensely voluptuous flavours. Among the châteaux that have profitably, if

A FAR CRY FROM THE GRANDER ESTATES OF BORDEAUX, CHÂTEAU VALANDRAUD BEGAN LIFE AS A PRIVATE GARAGE IN THE HEART OF ST ÉMILION. THE TINY AMOUNTS OF WINE IT PRODUCES ARE SOUGHT AFTER THROUGHOUT THE WORLD.

controversially, followed this route are Angélus (whose name refers to the fact that the bells from all three of St Émilion's churches can be heard there), Canon-la-Gaffelière (which, like La Gaffelière, is called after an old leper colony), Le Tertre-Roteboeuf and, most recently, Pavie, whose origins almost certainly date back to the Romans. For what it is worth, I have been far more convinced by the rich character of Angélus than by the jammy style of Pavie under a new owner at the beginning of the 21st century. Others disagree. Fans of more traditional St Émilions tend to prefer wines like Troplong-Mondot and Larmande, La Gaffelière and Clos Fourtet.

The lower-lying land to the west of the town used to be called "Les Graves-St-Émilion" in an effort to take on some of the prestige enjoyed by the vineyards on the other side of the Garonne. The only problem, as the owner of Château Figeac, Thierry Manoncourt, forcibly pointed out, was that there wasn't nearly enough gravel to justify the name. The only significant deposits of crystal-quartz stones in this area form the *croupe* on which are situated his estate and Cheval Blanc. These two properties have a rivalry with deep roots. The former estate has the longer history, with a name that can be traced back to a Roman called Figeacus, a handsome manor house, parts of which date from the end of

the 16th century, and vineyards that were planted in the early 1700s. Cheval Blanc, which, according to local legend, is named after a post house where the wine-loving king Henri IV (who favoured white horses) used to change steeds, remained more or less unknown until a century later. Indeed, in 1832 its wine was still being sold as *vin de Figeac*, but its fortunes began to rise in 1852, when it fell in the form of a dowry into the hands of a man called Jean Laussac-Fourcaud, who promptly proceeded to double production to around 5,000 cases and to make wines good enough to win medals in competitions in Paris and London. Meanwhile, Château Figeac went into a decline under a succession of careless or absentee owners, which only came to a halt when Manoncourt took it over from his father in 1947. By that time, however, Cheval Blanc was well on its way to being recognized as one of the finest wines in France; its 1947 features on most lists of the greatest wines ever to have been produced. As for Figeac, today it is considered to be the St Émilion equivalent of a Médoc "Super-Second" (see p.131).

The rivals are a curious pair because neither is a truly typical St Émilion, but nor do they resemble the Pomerols from adjoining vineyards. The various gravels of the *croupe* suit Cabernet grapes better than the Merlot with which St Émilion is usually associated. So, Cheval

III

CHÂTEAU FIGEAC (ABOVE) WAS ONCE FAR MORE FAMOUS
THAN ITS NEIGHBOUR CHÂTEAU CHEVAL BLANC (RIGHT).
BOTH ARE SET APART FROM THE REST OF ST ÉMILION BY
THE GRAVEL *CROUPE* ON WHICH THEIR VINES ARE GROWN.

Blanc offers a unique showcase for the Cabernet Franc
grape, which forms two thirds of the blend and helps to
make a wine that is both supremely elegant and yet far
more approachable than the great wines of the Médoc.
At Figeac, the Merlot also represents a third, but here
the Cabernets Sauvignon and Franc share equal
honours. I have always been seduced by Cheval Blanc
and often pleasurably perplexed by the neither-quite-
Médoc-nor-quite-St-Émilion style of Figeac, which can
be a very difficult wine to assess in its youth.

The dividing line between these St Émilion châteaux and some of the best estates of Pomerol is as hard to discern as the boundary between the villages of Burgundy or between St Julien and Pauillac. Vieux-Château-Certan and Châteaux Beauregard, L'Évangile, Petit-Village and La Conseillante are all a short stroll away, but their wines have a style that's all their own. Pomerol is the most hedonistic wine in Bordeaux. The combination of the *crasse de fer* – ironstone – soil and the Merlot (which represents 60 to 80 per cent of the blend at most châteaux) and Cabernet Franc grapes makes for flavours of black cherries, plums and Dundee cake, coupled with an earthy mineral note that should temper any tendency to jamminess. Sometimes there are spicy fireworks too, but that usually has more to do with the winemaking than the soil or the grapes.

Surprisingly, these exotic wines are produced on a mostly flat, featureless slab of vine-covered landscape with only an oddly dominant church spire and the occasional, often quite modest, château to add a note of interest to the horizon. Drive through the vineyards to take a closer look at the village surrounding that church and you are in for a disappointment; all you will find is a building incongruously hosting – when I was last there at least – the local judo club, and a few nondescript houses. At first sight, there seems to be no justification at all for the size of the church; the village of Catusseau and the surrounding hamlets seem unlikely to have had enough worshippers to fill its pews. A clue lies in the Maltese crosses that abound in the *appellation*: the Maltese cross is the symbol of the Knights of Malta, previously known as the Knights of St John of Jerusalem, who used to stop here on their way to Santiago de Compostela.

One of the crosses that has attracted the most notice is in the grounds of Château Beauregard, which, though built in 1795 to a design by a pupil of Victor Louis, architect of the Grand Théâtre, stands close to the site of an important 12th-century *manoir*. Beauregard, with its parkland, moat and the square towers that give form to a stone balustraded terrace, is not only one of the most striking buildings in all of Bordeaux; it is also the model for a mansion called Mille-Fleurs which was built in the early 1930s on Long Island for the millionairess widow of Harry Guggenheim. All the replica lacks is the sandstone walls – the American version is in brick – and, of course, the wines.

But neat vineyards are a relative novelty in Pomerol. Until the second half of the 18th century, most of the land was worked by tenant farmers who would have grown – mostly white – grapes among a wide range of other crops. The switch to serious winemaking came at

THE QUIET, HISTORICALLY OVERLOOKED REGION OF POMEROL HAS ENJOYED A HEYDAY SINCE THE 1980s, ALLOWING ESTATES
SUCH AS CHÂTEAU ROUGET (ABOVE) TO INVEST IN EXPENSIVE NEW WINERY BUILDINGS AND EQUIPMENT.

Château Trochau (later called Tropchaud) in 1750 when a pioneer called Louis Fontémoing tore up his white vines, drained the land and planted Cabernet and Malbec. His lead was followed over the ensuing decades by a doughty woman called Madame Conseillan who used the profits from dealing in metals to establish La Conseillante, and by the owners of châteaux Certan, Nenin, Gazin, Pétrus and Trotanoy (then called Trop-Ennuie – "too much bother"). Over much of the next century, although fine wines were made, the region from which they came went largely unrecognized; Pomerol was still being treated as part of St Émilion.

THIS UNPREPOSSESSING COTTAGE IN POMEROL (ABOVE) IS HOME TO LE PIN, ONE OF THE PRICIEST WINES IN BORDEAUX.
CHÂTEAU PÉTRUS (OPPOSITE) IS A LITTLE MORE IMPOSING, BUT MIGHT GO UNNOTICED IF IT WEREN'T FOR ITS SIGN.

The top châteaux – Pétrus, Vieux-Château-Certan and Trotanoy – began to develop a following in northern France and Belgium, but even in the early 20th century, the prices they commanded were still often lower than those paid for quite humble Médocs and St Émilions. Crucially too, the quantities they produced were – as they are today – relatively tiny, with roughly 3,500 cases for Pétrus and 6,000 for Beauregard compared to the 20,000 or more of a top Médoc estate like Latour or Lafite. Pomerol is the smallest of Bordeaux's quality *appellations*, with vineyards that cover around a seventh of the area of St Émilion. Largely for these reasons, no one ever thought it worth classifying the vineyards here, and, even now, they produce the priciest unclassified wines in France.

The present success of Pomerol owes much to three very different men. First, there was Jean-Pierre Moueix, the Libourne merchant I mentioned earlier, whose family firm – now headed by his son Christian – owns, or is responsible for the quality of, such properties as La Fleur-Pétrus, Lagrange, Magdelaine, Trotanoy and,

most crucially, Pétrus. It was the small quantities of immediately accessible but long-lived, exotically deep, almost pure Merlot produced by the deceptively undistinguished-looking château at the end of this list that – for many people – first brought sex appeal to Bordeaux.

Second, there was the writer and critic Robert Parker who introduced large numbers of American baby-boomers to Bordeaux in general and the rich, ripe, immediate pleasures of the Merlot grape in particular. And lastly, there was a man called Michel Rolland who owns Château Le Bon Pasteur and, more importantly, acts with his wife Dany as consultant to numerous estates here, helping them to make the kinds of ripe wine that are appreciated by Robert Parker and the readers of his newsletter, *The Wine Advocate*. Thanks to these men, to the efforts of the owners of starry properties such as Clinet, L'Évangile (which belongs to the Rothschilds of Lafite), Lafleur and Vieux-Château-Certan, and to the instant global fame of Jacques Thienpont's minuscule Château Le Pin, the *appellation* of Pomerol has developed a magnetic pull on wine lovers across the world.

117

CHAPTER SEVEN

NORTHWARD FROM POMEROL

Tucked away to the north, east and west of Pomerol, regions such as Bourg, Fronsac and

the Côtes de Castillon ring few bells among modern wine lovers. Historically, though,

these were the source of some of the most sought-after wine in Bordeaux. But if they are

rich in history, these *appellations* and the Côtes des Francs, Lalande de Pomerol and the so-

called "satellites" of St Émilion can also boast some of the best value in the region: wines

produced with as much or more care than those in many a better-known part of Bordeaux.

THE BATTLE OF CASTILLON, COMMEMORATED BY THIS SIGN (ABOVE) MARKED THE END OF THE HUNDRED YEARS' WAR AND
THE DEPARTURE OF THE ENGLISH. THE CHÂTEAU DU BOUILH (OPPOSITE) IS ONE OF THE MAJOR ESTATES IN BOURG.

S tars rise and stars fall. The regions of Fronsac, Castillon and Bourg were once among the leading names in Bordeaux. Today, they lurk in the shadows cast by the Médoc, Pessac-Léognan, St Émilion and Pomerol. Indeed, even the Bordelais themselves seem sometimes to forget that these areas belong to their team. On a recent visit to a supermarket in Pauillac, I found that the only example of wine from Fronsac had been carefully placed on a shelf alongside the Corbières and Minervois from way down south in Languedoc-Roussillon; in a small restaurant in Bordeaux, the wine list included a Côtes de Castillon among "other regions of France" along with Côtes du Rhône. If this lack of historic respect seems a little unfair, it does at least offer an advantage to wine drinkers. The often-overlooked vineyards that surround Pomerol and St Émilion can be among the best places to go looking for bargains.

The best way to begin such a quest is by crossing a little stream called the Barbanne (see map, p.99), which separates Pomerol from the "satellite" region of Lalande de Pomerol, and climbing through some woods, past

THE 14TH-CENTURY CHÂTEAU DE MONBADON IN THE CÔTES DE FRANCS, A REGION THAT, UNTIL RECENTLY, HAS BEEN WOEFULLY UNDER-APPRECIATED. HOWEVER, RECENT INVESTMENT BY OUTSIDERS IS NOW PAYING DIVIDENDS.

the sleepy hamlet of Néac, to a slightly higher plateau beyond. Lalande de Pomerol has estates whose history goes back to the early days of the last millennium. The vineyards of châteaux Vieux-Cardinal-Lafaurie and Haut-Chaigneau in Néac were both producing wine in the 12th century, and local records show the monks tending their vines at the latter estate's neighbour, Château Canon-Chaigneau. As in Pomerol, most of the 200 or so estates here have modest buildings and small vineyards. But there are exceptions, such as Château Moncets with its pair of slate-roofed square towers,

Siaurac, Tournefeuille and — my own favourite — the handsome 17th-century Château Perron. As for the wines, these vary widely depending on the soil in which the vines are planted. The best, richest wines come from the east, close to Néac, where the clay helps to make for rich Pomerol-like flavours. Châteaux closer to the little village of Lalande de Pomerol have sandier soil and make wines with less personality.

The Barbanne also separates St Émilion from its closest so-called "satellites", St-Georges-St-Émilion and Montagne-St-Émilion, but the countryside here is

THE CHÂTEAU ST-GEORGES IN ST-GEORGES-ST-ÉMILION IS ONE OF THE MOST BEAUTIFUL BUILDINGS IN BORDEAUX. ITS WINES ARE IMPRESSIVE TOO: A MATCH FOR MANY A WINE FROM THE SUPPOSEDLY CLASSIER *APPELLATION* OF ST ÉMILION.

quite different. This is quite wild, hilly territory patterned with small vineyards. Among them, overlooking the neat ranks of its vines, stands one of the finest buildings in all of Bordeaux, Château St-Georges, which was built in 1770 by Victor Louis, architect of the Grand Théâtre in Bordeaux. If the rich, plummy-berryish wine here were as distinguished as the château, it would outclass Cheval Blanc. It isn't quite that good — none of the wines in the Satellites is — but, like all of the best efforts in the hills, it's far better than many of the St Émilion Grands Crus whose style it shares. Along with Château St-André-Corbin, this is one of the few estates to use the St-Georges-St-Émilion *appellation*; most prefer to be sold as Montagne-St-Émilion, alongside such wines as châteaux Faizeau (which belongs to the owners of La Croix de Gay in Pomerol), Reclos, Teyssier and Rouzeau (which is under the same ownership as Château Balestard-la-Tonnelle in St Émilion). Apart from its château, St Georges boasts another landmark, in the shape of a 12th-century church which would have welcomed pilgrims as they passed through the region. Those seeking an alternative place of

123

THE ÉGLISE ST JEAN IN LALANDE DE FRONSAC DATES FROM THE 11TH AND 12TH CENTURIES. ITS TYMPANUM, REPRESENTING THE VISION OF ST JOHN, IS ONE OF THE MOST REMARKABLE PIECES OF MEDIEVAL STONEMASONRY IN THE REGION.

worship could, instead, head for Montagne, which has a Romanesque church with memorable carvings over its door, as well as the immense medieval Château des Tours, whose name refers to the towers at each of its four corners.

Lussac-St-Émilion, setting for an annual so-called "international" barrel-rolling triathlon, is producing increasingly impressive wines (such as châteaux Cap de Merle and Lyonnat), as is Puisseguin-St-Émilion, whose Celtic name means "hill with the strong wine". (Branda and Vieux-Château-Guibeau are among the stars here.) After various tastings, I am far from sure that the wines of the individual Satellite *appellations* have established recognizable identities of their own, but I do know that, taken as a whole, this is one of the areas of Bordeaux where some of the greatest efforts are being made. Just as they are in the Côtes de Francs, where vines may well

have been grown by the Romans. The visitable Château de Francs, close to the little village of the same name, was built in stages between the 12th and 17th centuries and surrounds an attractive grassy courtyard. Of the berryish wines here, I'd recommend La Prade, Marsau, La Claverie and Puygueraud.

If, throughout their history, the Bordelais generally did their utmost to avoid getting into a fight themselves, preferring to focus their attention on trading with as many different parties as possible, the land on which they lived was often the setting for battles between others. None of these fights came close to competing with the one at Castillon on July 17th 1453, when the French army under Charles VII defeated the English troops led by Sir John Talbot, Earl of Shrewsbury. The victory marked the end of the Hundred Years' War, and the end of English occupation of Aquitaine. The handsome, old,

L'Hôtel de Ville — the Town Hall — of Castillon-la-Bataille (above) stands as a reminder of the historic importance of this river port whose name recalls the battle that ended the Hundred Years' War. The wines from these Côtes de Castillon vines (opposite) would once have been sold as basic Bordeaux.

These steep vineyard slopes in Fronsac (above) are unusual in Bordeaux. They are among the oldest in the region. The historic Bastide of Blaye (opposite) covers 18 hectares and was built on the ruins of a Roman fort as part of a defensive chain designed by the architect Vauban for Louis XIV.

partially walled town that is now called Castillon-la-Bataille in memory of that encounter also recalls its own history as a major river port. Its wines, which were once sold as Bordeaux Supérieur, often now compete with those of St Émilion – if for no other reason than the fact that owners of St Émilion estates are investing in vineyards here. Châteaux La-Roche-Beaulieu, Pitray, Faugères and Robin are all worth looking out for.

Generally more impressive than the Côtes de Castillon, Fronsac and Canon-Fronsac to the west of Libourne have some of the steepest vineyards and the oldest vinous reputations in Bordeaux. Before

Libourne grew to dominate the trade along the Dordogne, Fronsac was a major port, generating sufficient wealth to warrant the building of castles like the the 13th-century Château La Rivière, which now looks like a setting for an old Polanski film and stands above a maze of cellars dug into the hillside. Over the following 600 years, Fronsac's wines remained among the most sought after in the Libournais. In the mid-19th century, the German merchant Wilhelm Franck listed no fewer than eight Fronsac properties in his *Traité*; Pomerol warranted just one. The prosperity engendered during that period can still be sensed in the old

WINEMAKERS TAKE GREATER CARE THAN EVER TO VERIFY THE QUALITY OF THEIR WINES. EXPERTS IN LABORATORIES SUCH AS OENOLOGIE IN BOURG (ABOVE LEFT) ANALYZE WINES BEFORE BOTTLING. THIS ARCH (ABOVE RIGHT) WAS CUT INTO THE ROCK IN BOURG FROM WHOSE JETTY (OPPOSITE) WINE HAS BEEN SHIPPED SINCE THE EARLIEST DAYS OF BORDEAUX.

merchants' houses that are to be seen in the quiet riverside village of Fronsac itself.

Finally, heading north along the right bank of the Dordogne and Gironde, we get to Prignac-et-Marcamps where there is a cave decorated with prehistoric wall paintings that reveal this to be one of the oldest-known settlements in the region. If ancient man found this area to be an ideal place to hunt bison and mammoths, the Romans appreciated Bourg — a little closer to the sea — as a good spot to establish a fort that commanded access to the river, a port and some vineyards. Today, as you walk down through the various levels of the walled town to the water, it is easy to see from the houses how significant a place this once was. Even so, it is hard to imagine that Bourg once handled more river traffic than Bordeaux itself. In recent times, the red and white wines of the Côtes de Bourg have been thought to have greater potential than they have actually shown; sadly, a lack of ambition and skill on the part of the owners has prevented most from producing

anything better than basic Bordeaux. The exceptions to the rule are wines like Château Tayac and Château Roc de Cambes, which belongs to the owner of Le Tertre-Roteboeuf in St Émilion.

Blaye, about a dozen kilometres further north, is another under-exploited area and merely confuses matters by having three separate *appellations*: Blaye, Côtes de Blaye and Premières Côtes de Blaye. The first two of these are more or less interchangeable – except for the fact that Côtes de Blaye is exclusively white. Premières Côtes de Blaye, which comes in both colours, should ideally be a little fuller in flavour and ripeness. An indication of what can be achieved on the hillsides here is to be found in the excellent whites of Haut-Bertinerie, the reds of La Tonnelle and Haut-Sociando and the "garage" wine Passion du Prieuré Malesan, but standards are generally slightly lower than in Bourg, and the wines somewhat lighter in body. Even if there were no wine on offer, however, Blaye would have little difficulty in justifying its existence. Quite apart from a major tourist attraction in the shape of the huge, sprawling 17th-century *citadelle* which stands on the site of a fort originally built by the Romans (who named the settlement Blavia), there is a busy port from which ferries regularly cross to Lamarque in the Médoc. All Bourg and Blaye need to step out of the shadows is for a few more producers to adopt the self-belief that is so prevalent on the other side of the river.

129

CHOOSING WINE IN BORDEAUX

Choosing and buying a bottle of Bordeaux can be a little like setting out on a journey with a set of incomplete and often mutually contradictory maps. The one covering the region's nearly five dozen *appellations* should at least give you an appoximate idea of the style of wine you are likely to get. Reds from the "right bank" of the Gironde and Dordogne (principally the *appellations* of St Émilion, Pomerol, the satellites and Castillon, Bourg, Blaye and Fronsac) rather than the left (the Médoc and Graves, in particular) will be more influenced by the softer, plummier Merlot than the more tannic and blackcurranty Cabernet Sauvignon. Focusing in greater detail, you should be able to discern a specific character that the particular soil, aspects and grape varieties have collectively given to each particular *appellation*.

These character traits can allow a skilled taster to identify the *appellation* of a wine he or she has never tasted before, but there are exceptions. A growing number of winemakers are transcending their *appellation* by

changing their viticultural and winemaking techniques. Some modern "garage" St Émilions, for example, are so spicy, super-ripe and oaky that they might almost be mistaken for a wine from the Rhône or Australia.

Appellations can be very confusing. Château Mouton-Rothschild's red wine is a Pauillac while its white, like every other white from the Médoc, may only legally be sold as Bordeaux Blanc. The Château du Seuil, close to the River Garonne, legally produces five separate *appellations* from the same vineyards: red Bordeaux and Premières Côtes de Bordeaux, and three whites: a sweet Cérons, a Graves and a Bordeaux Blanc. A regional *appellation* can in any case never provide a guarantee of quality. The vineyards with the best soil in St Émilion are officially recognized as "Grand Cru", but there are plenty of carelessly made wines here that compare poorly with the efforts of more quality-conscious châteaux whose land does not have Grand Cru status. The suffix "Supérieur" on a red Bordeaux should indicate that it has been produced from riper grapes, but

the skill and care with which those grapes have been turned into wine will still vary so widely from one label to another that many good estates and merchants prefer not to use it.

The Bordelais themslves have attempted to separate the sheep from the goats over the years by drawing up sets of classifications. Unfortunately, there is little consistency in the way this has been done. The Médoc and Sauternes still live by lists of "Crus Classés" – "classed growths" – dating back to 1855 when the Médoc was split into five layers of quality and Sauternes into three. The only Graves château to be classified in 1855 was Château Haut-Brion. The rest of Graves had to wait until 1953 (for the reds) and 1959 (for the whites). There are no levels of classification here. Graves wines – red or white – are either classified growths (Crus Classés) or they are not.

The Médoc, Graves and Sauternes classifications have one thing in common: apart from the promotion of Château Mouton-Rothschild from second to first growth in 1973 (explained as the correction of an historic error), they have all been cast in stone, despite the fact that châteaux have been bought and sold and, in a few cases, such as Château Peixotto, ceased to exist as independent entities. More crucially, their owners may have expanded their vineyards and now be making wine from vines that had nothing to do with the château when it was assessed a century and a half ago. Or they may be trying harder – or less hard – than they used to. Châteaux Rauzan-Gassies and Rauzan-Ségla are neighbouring estates in Margaux that are both officially classified as second growths. Rauzan-Ségla deserves its position (though it didn't in the 1970s), while Rauzan-Gassies might nowadays justifiably be demoted to a fifth growth. There are several châteaux, such as Chasse-Spleen, Potensac, Angludet and Sociando-Mallet, that failed to be included in the 1855 classification but are now making wine that matches Rauzan-Gassies. These supposedly sub-Cru Classé estates come under the heading of "Crus Bourgeois" – a Médoc designation whose members classified their wines in 2003. Also looking for

promotion – but at the other end of the classification – is a set of châteaux dubbed the "Super-Seconds" that regularly outperform their peers. Including such top-quality second growths as Léoville-Lascases, Léoville-Barton, Pichon-Longueville-Baron, Pichon-Longueville-Comtesse-Lalande, Cos d'Estournel and Ducru-Beaucaillou, the group confusingly also encompasses lower-ranking châteaux such as the third-growth Palmer and the fifth-growth Lynch-Bages.

St Émilion has managed its affairs rather better, drawing up a classification in 1955 that is now revised every decade. Under-performers are demoted and estates that consistently make better wine can climb the ladder. But there is confusion here too – between these "Grands Crus Classés" and the "Grands Crus" that owe their status to the quite separate regional *appellation* of Grand Cru St Émilion. Meanwhile, Pomerol gets along very nicely without any official classification at all.

The key word here, though, is official, because anyone wanting to buy Bordeaux has plenty of unofficial, independent sources of advice to choose from in the shape of individual critics. In France, the best informed critic is Michel Bettane, whose *Classement* (written annually with Thierry Deseauve), like the *Guide Michelin*, gives favoured wine producers one, two or three stars. In the US – and globally – the most influential voice is that of Robert Parker, whose books on Bordeaux have been translated into countless languages. Parker describes châteaux he likes as Good, Very Good, Excellent or Outstanding and gives their wines scores from 50 to 100. The British critic Clive Coates prefers to rate wines

131

out of 20. Jancis Robinson and Steve Tanzer are other critics whose opinions I respect. Magazines such as *Decanter*, *La Revue du Vin de France*, the *Wine Spectator* and *International Wine* (of which I am publishing editor) all offer recommendations and background information — as do specialist merchants. My advice is to follow the same rules you would when buying shares: take the trouble to look beyond a single source of advice.

Where the critics and merchants differ from the official classifications is in their ability to assess the quality and style of wine a château has made in a particular vintage. The climate varies widely in Bordeaux, with some years being far cooler and rainier than others. The weather sometimes favours particular parts of the region, allowing St Émilion's Merlots, for example, to make better wines than the Cabernets in the Médoc — or vice versa. Vintages that are great in Sauternes may be poor for red wine. As a rule, however, the more challenging the conditions, the greater the advantage of well-situated vineyards whose vines face the sun and grow on soil from which water drains easily. But it is not simply a matter of some vintages being better than others: there are years whose wines simply take more or less time to soften. Some "lesser" vintages are lighter and shorter-lived; others always have a mean, unripe flavour. However, nowadays more than ever, good producers skilfully manage to outshine their neighbours in bad years — possibly by discarding all but their very best vats. And that's the fascination of wine in general and Bordeaux in particular: it is not a cathedral or a painting to stand before and admire, but a hard-fought series of games to be followed moment by moment, bottle by bottle and glass by glass.

LE TERROIR

Ask a New World producer why a wine tastes the way it does, and he or she will probably reply with a list of factors, headed by the grape variety or varieties, followed by the climate and the skill and technique of the winemaker. As an afterthought, they might then remember to mention the soil in which the vines were grown. Now put the question to a Frenchman, and you might get a single word: *terroir*, for which, like the old English expression "breeding", there is no simple translation. Effectively, *le terroir* refers to a combination of the type or types of soil to be found in the vineyard and the microclimate (which could be affected by the angle and direction of a slope and nearby hills, woods or streams). The grape variety also can form part of *le terroir*, but the human factor does not. Revealingly, there is no commonly used French translation for the English word "winemaker" – instead, there are *vignerons* and *viticulteurs* (both terms for vinegrowers) and, in Bordeaux, *maîtres de chai*: cellarmasters.

If the Frenchman tends to overlook winemaking technique, he expects to find the flavour of the mineral constituents of the gravel or limestone soil. He would acknowledge the blackcurrant flavour of the Cabernet grapes or the plum and cherry of the Merlot, but these would be no more than the principal instruments in an orchestral arrangement, and certainly less important than the character of the vineyard. Indeed, for Jean Delmas, of Château Haut-Brion, the hint of soil should dominate the grape rather than vice versa.

French traditionalists believe that mentioning a grape variety on the label distracts attention from the place a wine was made. And they wince at praise being given to modern Bordeaux wines that are said to taste like California Cabernets or wines from the Rhône or Burgundy. In their view, authenticity and typicity are valued more highly than pleasure. Elsewhere, pleasure often comes first. My own view is pitched midway between the two camps. I too relish the subtle but discernible differences between classic wines from the neighbouring communes of Pauillac and St Julien, but would frankly prefer to drink a tasty atypical Bordeaux than one whose genuineness merely accentuates the negative qualities that can be found in this region's less successful wines.

THE SOIL

You don't have to be a gardener or a geologist to notice the differences in soil type that distinguish one part of Bordeaux from another. In the Médoc and Graves, the best vineyards, such as those of châteaux Margaux and Haut-Brion, are covered with pale grey gravel – literally, *les graves* – which drains well and is ideal for the Cabernet Sauvignon (see photograph, p.134). In St Émilion and Pomerol, by contrast, the soil is obviously heavier, and better suited to the Merlot and Cabernet Franc. Even within a single *appellation*, however, there are areas that stand out from their surroundings. In St Émilion, châteaux Cheval Blanc and Figeac, for example, are both on a *croupe* – a low, gravelly ridge that is quite unlike the flatter, more clayey soil of their neighbours. For this reason, the two estates' wines include

133

a higher proportion of Cabernet grapes. Other, less illustrious St Émilion vineyards are situated on flat, sandy terrain that never produces top-class wine.

THE GRAPES
While red Bordeaux in particular is — with rare exceptions — made from blends of different types of grape, the precise recipe (the *assemblage*) varies from château to château and vintage to vintage, depending on the soil, the style the producer is aiming for and the way each variety has reacted to the climate of that season. Over the years, too, some varieties become almost extinct in Bordeaux while others gain in precedence. Nineteenth-century lists of grapes included Carmenère and Tarney Coulant, which no longer exist here. Malbec (now almost never used in top wines) was a basic ingredient in Bordeaux, while (the now ubiquitous) Merlot and the (now quite illegal) Syrah were both "complementary" varieties used to make up for failings in other grapes.

Cabernet Sauvignon
The acknowledged king of Bordeaux

grapes is actually a newcomer, having only been cultivated in the Médoc since the early 19th century, almost 2,000 years after its genetic parent, the Cabernet Franc, is thought to have arrived from Albania. It is, though, in the gravelly soil of this part of Bordeaux, where it usually makes up 40 to 50% of the blend, and in the Graves — where the figure is often closer to 60% — that it develops its most majestic blackcurrant-and-cedar flavours. The Cabernet Sauvignon also appreciates a climate that, in

the best vintages, is neither warm enough to give the wines a jammy, overripe character, nor cool enough to give them a leafy "green" flavour. The tannin that contributes to the longevity of Cabernet Sauvignon-based Bordeaux can be another concern, which explains why producers here generally soften what might otherwise be overly tough wine by having Merlot grapes constitute a quarter to a third of the blend. The remainder of the *assemblage* tends to be made up with Cabernet Franc and, in some cases, Petit Verdot. The Cabernet Sauvignon grape is more rarely used in St Émilion and Pomerol but it can feature there (usually in proportions of around 10%) where there are patches of gravel.

Merlot
A variety that has a name with two easy-to-pronounce syllables and supple, plummy and easy-to-enjoy flavours — especially within a few years of the harvest. The Merlot ripens earlier than the Cabernet Sauvignon, and performs better on the heavier soils of regions such as St Émilion and Pomerol where the latter grape generally finds it hard

to ripen at all. Unless it is well handled, the Merlot can, however, produce wines that are thin and weedy or dull and earthy. The near 100% Merlot Bordeaux, such as Pétrus and Le Pin, are historically exceptions to the rule; most St Émilions and Pomerols are blended with Cabernet Franc and, to a far lesser extent, Cabernet Sauvignon. Wines such as Angélus, Ausone, and Vieux-Château-Certan contain only 50 to 60% Merlot, and the grape typically constitutes a mere third of the blend of Cheval Blanc, most critics' top St Émilion. The style of Merlot-influenced wines depends greatly on the ripeness of the grapes when they are picked; the later the harvest, the richer and more spicy and fruitcakey the flavour – but also the less subtle and refined. Mahler versus Mozart.

Cabernet Franc

Apart from its contribution to Cheval Blanc, where it forms two thirds of the blend, this is Bordeaux's supporting actor par excellence. While the Merlot and Cabernet Sauvignon are hogging the limelight here and elsewhere, the Cabernet Franc's only claim to fame

outside the region is in Chinon and Bourgueil in the Loire. In Bordeaux it usefully combines attributes of both the Cabernet Sauvignon (flavours of blackcurrant and mint) and Merlot (earlier ripening, tolerance for clay soils and softer tannins), without usually rising to the heights that can be achieved by these varieties. Often the third most used variety in the wines of the Médoc, it comes into its own in St Émilion where it is the ideal partner for the Merlot

Petit Verdot

The vital ingredient in many a Médoc blend and once much more widely used here, the Petit Verdot has a spicy, peppery note that is never found in the Cabernets or the Merlot. Curiously, producers give very different reports on this grape; one saying that it rarely ripens, while a neighbour happily adds 2 to 8% to his wine every year. The answer to this puzzle is that there are two different clones of the variety, one of which ripens more easily than the other. The better clone is helping the Petit Verdot to make a comeback, although not in Pomerol, where it is still illegal.

Sauvignon Blanc

The sole ingredient of much basic dry white Bordeaux, this bright, blackcurrant-leafy variety is also usually the predominant variety for classier dry whites – Smith-Haut-Lafitte and Couhins-Lurton include up to 98 to 100%. Some great wines, however, include rather less: Haut-Brion and Pape-Clément Blanc, for example, have just 45%. It also takes a secondary role in the sweet wines of Sauternes and Barsac. Look out for its smokier cousin the Sauvignon Gris, which is still rare but proving increasingly popular.

Semillon

Much trickier to handle than the Sauvignon Blanc, the potentially deliciously peachy Semillon needs skilled winemaking to avoid taking on a dull earthy character. Its contribution to a dry blend can vary from near zero to 70% (Laville-Haut-Brion). Its forte, though, is in sweet wines, thanks to its susceptibility to noble rot – the benign fungus integral to the making of all great Sauternes. For these wines, the proportion of Semillon is between 75% (Coutet) and 100% (Climens), with 80 to 85% being common.

135

DIRECTORY OF RECOMMENDED CHÂTEAUX

BARSAC

Climens Typical of the Barsac *appellation*, this estate produces wines that seem to be a little more delicate than their neighbours in Sauternes — but just as fine and long-lived.

CANON-FRONSAC

Canon de Brem A leading property in an underrated region that once enjoyed greater fame. Fine, Merlot-based wine.

CÔTES DE BOURG

Roc de Cambes A star in what can be a rustic *appellation*. Well-made, Merlot-influenced wines with some subtlety.

CÔTES DE CASTILLON

Clarière-Laithwaite Made by an English wine merchant, this is a plummy, Merlot-based wine that has beaten far pricier neighbours in blind tastings.

CÔTES DE FRANCS

Puygueraud If you are looking for high quality inexpensive red Bordeaux, this estate, owned by the Thienpont family of Le Pin, Vieux-Château-Certan and Labégorce-Zédé, is for you.

ENTRE-DEUX-MERS

Bonnet One of the most beautiful châteaux in Bordeaux and home to the Lurton family who own classier estates such as La Louvière, this is a source of keenly priced, reliable dry white Entre-Deux-Mers and good red Bordeaux.

La Tour-Mirambeau Rivalling Château Bonnet as a star in this region, La Tour-Mirambeau regularly produces delicious, creamy dry white.

FRONSAC

Dalem This is classic Fronsac at its very best, with the plummy flavour of the Merlot tempered by a wild raspberry character. Fairly priced and well worth keeping.

La Dauphine One of the flagships of Fronsac; immediately appealing, Merlot-dominant wines with just enough new oak.

La Rivière A spooky hillside château replete with caves, this looks like the setting for a Polanski film. The wines, especially a new prestige *cuvée*, are mulberryish and rich.

Vieille-Cure One of the modern stalwarts of the Fronsac *appellation*, this property benefits from investment by its American owners and professional advice from the ubiquitous Michel Rolland of Le Bon Pasteur.

GRAVES
Cardaillan Graves reds are often overlooked nowadays in the quest for bigger, richer fare, but this is quintessential light-bodied inexpensive red Bordeaux.

Clos Floridène With a reputation for producing top-class dry white in the 19th century, this is a modern beacon of quality thanks to the efforts of owner-winemaker-guru-consultant-academic Denis Dubourdieu.

HAUT MÉDOC
Beaumont A source of modern, generally good-value Médoc from an estate that is under the same ownership as Château Beychevelle.

Cantemerle Near La Lagune, this beautiful château, set in a private wood, is to the south of most other classed growths. Its wines are lighter than many and stand comparison with pricier fare from nearby Margaux.

La Lagune A beautiful estate that is unusual in being a classed growth that is not within one of the Médoc *appellation*s such as Margaux or St Julien.

Lamarque Despite the fairytale medieval appearance of the château, the wine here is well-made modern Médoc for relatively early drinking.

Sociando-Mallet One of the stars of the Crus Bourgeois — and an estate that would easily qualify as a fourth or fifth growth if ever the 1855 Classification were to be updated.

LALANDE DE POMEROL
Fleur de Bouard A new star from the owners of Château Angélus, this offers the cherry and chocolate flavours of top-class Pomerol — at a more affordable price.

LISTRAC
Clarke A major investment by a branch of the Rothschild family linked to neither Mouton-Rothschild nor Lafite. Recently much more approachable in its youth since the proportion of Merlot was increased.

Fourcas-Hosten Classic Listrac with an initially daunting toughness, this château makes unfashionable wines that repay ageing.

137

LOUPIAC

Ricaud A rival to many in Sauternes, this château produces sweet wines with wonderful luscious flavours.

MARGAUX

d'Angludet A Cru Bourgeois under the same winemaking regime as Château Palmer. Fine value wines with typical blackberryish Margaux character.

La Gurgue A Cru Bourgeois with vineyards close to those of Château Margaux. Often produces Cru Classé-quality wines with typical, perfumed Margaux style.

Labégorce-Zédé A Cru Bourgeois belonging to the Thienpont family (of Le Pin and Vieux-Château-Certan fame), with a strong following among those looking for fairly priced, classy Médoc wines.

Margaux The ultimate Bordeaux? Fine, intense, blackberryish and blackcurranty wine which has the perfume that sets the best wines of this *appellation* apart from their neighbours. The Pavillon Rouge "second wine" and Pavillon Blanc white are brilliant too.

Monbrison A regular favourite among Margaux fans looking for value, this Cru Bourgeois often outclasses some classed growths.

Palmer Officially ranked as only a third growth, this is definitely a "Super Second". Fine, perfumed wines that often overtake others over the long haul.

Rauzan-Ségla A fine "Super Second", following a period in the shadows in the 1970s. Now annually putting its neighbour Rauzan-Gassies to shame

with its impressively made modern, yet classic, wines.

MÉDOC

Potensac Under the same ownership as Château Léoville Lascases but costing a fraction of the price, this Cru Bourgeois estate offers a great example of top class winemaking in a less than top class part of the Médoc.

La Tour-Haut-Caussan A very reliable Cru Bourgeois with rich blackcurranty Cabernet Sauvignon flavours and well-judged contact with new oak.

MONTAGNE-ST-ÉMILION

Faizeau One of the stars of the St Émilion "satellites", this hillside estate belongs to the same family as La Croix de Gay in Pomerol. Immediately enjoyable Merlot-based wines of St Émilion Grand Cru standard.

Roudier Fine St Émilion quality at a lower price: everything one looks for in this hilly satellite *appellation*.

MOULIS

Chasse-Spleen The most famous estate in Moulis-en-Médoc – and one of the Crus Bourgeois that is most likely to beat its Crus Classés neighbours in blind tastings. Classic berryish red Bordeaux.

Poujeaux Source of of the most reliable and immediately attractive examples of Moulis.

PAUILLAC

Haut-Bages-Libéral Under the same ownership as La Gurgue and Chasse-Spleen, this offers a taste of the blackcurrant-pastille flavour of Pauillac at a lower cost than most of its neighbours.

Lafite-Rothschild The Médoc at its best. Not always the most obvious wine in its youth, this can be the finest example of a wine that really justifies the jargon terms of "complex" and "supremely elegant". A Chanel dress in a bottle.

Latour Still many Bordeaux enthusiasts' notion of the ultimate wine in the region, because of its classic, long-lived character and the complexity that is rarely rivalled by showier, more fashionable wines from Pomerol and St Émilion.

Lynch-Bages Only officially recognized as a fifth growth, but generally regarded (and priced) as a "Super Second", this is one of the most reliable wines in the Médoc.

Mouton-Rothschild Always a little riper, richer and showier than Lafite and

Latour, Mouton sometimes seems to lack a little of those wines' subtlety. But in years such as 1945 and 1982 it is second to none.

Pichon-Longueville-Baron Sometimes outshining its neighbour, Pichon-Longueville-Comtesse-Lalande, this is a château that has benefited from huge investment in recent years.

Pichon-Longueville-Comtesse-Lalande Producer of gloriously come-hitherish but long-lived wine from vineyards next door to Latour. Now excitingly facing competition from Pichon-Longueville-Baron across the road.

Pontet-Canet Belonging to the same family as Lafon-Rochet in St Estèphe, this is a source of beautifully made, very typical Pauillac with great berry flavours.

PESSAC-LÉOGNAN

Carbonnieux One of the biggest estates in its *appellation*, and source of lovely, quite classic, red and white in which the "mineral" quality of the Graves and Pessac-Léognan shines through.

Domaine de Chevalier Hidden in a clearing among the woods and thus often a frost victim, this estate makes subtler, more raspberryish red wine than many now – and superlative white. Often a great success in poor vintages.

Haut-Bailly One of my favourite wines in this *appellation* – and one of the few estates here to make no white. Wines have lovely raspberry-mulberry flavours.

Haut-Brion Unique in Bordeaux in making one of the very top reds – and a great dry white. Quintessential traditional Graves with restrained power. Needs time to reveal its true potential.

La Louvière A flagship of the dynamic Lurton family – and one of the most reliable sources both for reds and whites in its *appellation*.

La Mission Haut-Brion Just across the road from Haut-Brion and sometimes rivalling it in the quality of its deep, black cherryish, perfumed red wine.

Laville-Haut-Brion Under the same winemaking regime as Haut-Brion, this is one of the ultimate expressions of the peachy flavours of great dry white Bordeaux.

Pape-Clément One of the oldest estates in Bordeaux now produces some of the most intense, oaky, modern wines.

Smith-Haut-Lafitte A relatively recent addition to the list of top Pessac-Léognan reds and whites – and one of the first estates to embrace organic winemaking. A rising star.

POMEROL

L'Évangile Under the same ownership as Lafite, and made to a similar standard. Less showy than some, but with wonderful intensity and potential for ageing.

La Fleur Pétrus Less concentrated than many nowadays, but still one of the most seductive wines in Bordeaux, with glorious, gently fragrant fruit character.

Le Pin First of the "garage" wines, and still made in tiny quantities in a dull-looking cottage. The wines are very rich and juicy in their youth but it is still

140

too early to judge how well they age. Stratospheric prices ignore this, however.

Pétrus The Merlot-lover's answer to the Cabernet fan's Latour and Lafite. Seductive and exotic wine that seems to have been made with spice and chocolate as well as grapes.

Trotanoy Rivalling its stable-mate Château Pétrus in its rich, cherry and spice qualities, this is still a very subtle wine compared to some of the showier "garage" efforts.

Vieux-Château-Certan More delicate than many, this Pomerol has more Cabernet character than most of its neighbours. It ages impeccably.

PREMIÈRES CÔTES
Carsin A Finnish-owned estate that has imported New World winemaking skills (and an Australian winemaker) to produce white wines in particular that put most of the neighbours to shame.

Lezongars A fast-rising star with intense, very modern, concentrated, oaky red wine.

SAUTERNES
Rieussec A contender for top rival to Yquem. Intense, yet perfectly balanced wines that deserve to be cellared for decades.

Suduiraut Impeccably rich wine that competes in terms of quality with châteaux Rieussec and Climens but beats them when it comes to intensity.

Yquem Huge, concentrated, majestic wine that is not released as early as its neighbours — and is not produced in every vintage. The ultimate sweet wine?

ST ÉMILION
Angélus A high flyer in its *appellation*, this is one of the best of the newer-wave St Émilions with plenty of complexity to support its intense fruit and oaky flavours.

Ausone The finest estate in St Émilion — and probably one of the oldest in Bordeaux. After a disappointing patch, performing especially well now, following the arrival of Michel Rolland as consultant.

Belair Next-door neighbour to Ausone, but made in a much gentler, more mineral, and essentially much more traditional style by Pascal Delbeck. Unfashionable, perhaps, but well worth ageing.

142

Canon Classic wine from an estate that went through a rocky patch in the 1980s. The style here leans toward subtlety rather than intensity.

Cheval Blanc Permanent contender for top Bordeaux, this estate is also the world's finest example of a wine made largely from Cabernet Franc. Beautiful long-lived wines that are at once subtle and powerful: the iron fist in the velvet glove.

Figeac Source of what can often be the hardest wine in Bordeaux to judge in its youth. This old estate's wines rarely quite match those of its neighbour Cheval Blanc, but they do tend to have wonderful, subtle ripe-fruit flavours.

La Fleur Classic, rather than powerfully modern, example of this *appellation* with a seductive perfumed character.

Magdelaine Less fashionable than some, but none the worse for that: fine, traditional, fragrant St Émilion with hidden strength.

Moulin St Georges Under the same ownership as Château Ausone, but much more affordable. Fine, quite classic wine with impressive candied-fruit flavours. Built to last.

Teyssier A British-owned estate that shows what careful winemaking can achieve in less than distinguished soil.

Troplong-Mondot A fine hillside estate producing wines that, under the guiding hand of owner Christine Valette, can have wonderful perfumed damson fruit character.

Valandraud The most famous "garage" wine in its *appellation* – and undeniably impressive in its intensity. Valandraud is not for lovers of traditional, "elegant" Médoc, but others find its spell irresistible.

ST ÉMILION GRAND CRU
Fombrauge One of the most reliable examples of St Émilion Grand Cru, with rich toffeeish Merlot character. Enjoyable young, these are worth keeping too.

ST ESTÈPHE
Calon-Ségur One of the trio of top St Estèphes, this château tends to produce wines that are typical of its *appellation*: initially quite tough, but packed with layers of blackcurrant flavour.

Cos d'Estournel Often mistaken for Pauillac, this "Super Second" estate is usually reckoned to be the best in its *appellation*. Gorgeous intense

dark-berry-flavoured wines whose spicy note recalls the oriental design of the building.

de Pez One of the oldest estates in the Médoc and now a high-flying Cru Bourgeois since its purchase in the 1990s by the owners of Louis Roederer Champagne.

Haut-Marbuzet One of the growing band of Crus Bourgeois that are better buys than some classed-growth Médocs. Intensely blackcurrant, modern wine.

Lafon-Rochet A rising star in its *appellation*, the well-made wines here have a lush quality that comes from a higher proportion of Merlot than some of its neighbours.

Montrose While its wines are sometimes overshadowed nowadays by the more immediately seductive efforts of Cos d'Estournel, Montrose produces some of the finest, longest-lived examples of St Estèphe.

Phélan-Ségur Rivalling de Pez, this is a fine example of modern St Estèphe, with rich fruit to match the inherent toughness of the *appellation*'s soil.

ST JULIEN
Branaire A producer of reliably good rather than showy wines that are typical of the cedary flavour of St Julien.

Ducru-Beaucaillou A "Super Second" château whose class wines are often underrated alongside the Pichons and Léovilles, but they are among the most long-lived classics in the Médoc.

Langoa-Barton Under the same ownership as Léoville-Barton, with wines that are made with the same care but are slightly lighter-bodied — and sold at a lower price.

Léoville-Barton One of the most fairly-priced "Super Seconds", with fine cedary flavour. A reliable buy in any vintage, and well worth cellaring for decades.

Léoville-Lascases The closest any contender gets to matching Lafite, Latour and Margaux on a consistent basis. Fine, intense, blackcurranty and built for the long haul.

Talbot Always a rich, juicy example of St Julien, with cedary flavour to spare. The white is worth looking out for too.

STE CROIX DU MONT
Loubens A classic sweet wine to match many a Sauternes.

143

ACKNOWLEDGMENTS

Robert Joseph would like to thank countless Bordeaux château owners, wine merchants, enthusiasts and writers across the world for the time, knowledge and wine they all have generously shared with him.

His website can be visited at <www.robertjoseph-online.com>.

Max Alexander would like to thank Nicola Watts-Allison, Sean Allison and Sue and Bob Watts for their help in producing this book.

His website can be visited at <www.maxalexander.com>.

The publisher would like to thank the following photographic library for permission to reproduce its material
p.78: Anthony Blake/The Anthony Blake Picture Library, London

Captions to photographs pp.130–44
p.131: Cluster of road and château signs, Lucognac, Médoc
p.132 (left): Bunches of Semillon grapes
p.132 (centre): Close-up of Semillon grapes
p.132 (right): Cabernet Franc grapes
p.134: Section of gravelly soil, Château Olivier, Pessac-Léognan
p.144: Vines tended by the Domaine de Chevalier growing outside Bordeaux airport, Mérignac